CATCH CHUB

THE ANGLING TIMES LIBRARY

CATCH CHUB

WITH

JOHN WILSON

Boxtree

IN ASSOCIATION WITH
ANGLING TIMES

First published in the UK 1991
by BOXTREE LIMITED, 36 Tavistock Street,
London WC2E 7PB

1 3 5 7 9 10 8 6 4 2

(text and photographs) John Wilson 1991
(illustrations) Boxtree Limited 1991

Angling Times is a weekly newspaper produced by EMAP
Publishing Limited, Bretton, Peterborough. Established in
1953, it is Britain's biggest selling weekly fishing publica-
tion. Every week it offers authoritative expert news, views
and advice on all aspects of coarse, sea and game fishing.
On sale every Wednesday.

Illustrations by David Batten
Cover design by Dave Goodman/Millions Design
Design by Peter Ward

Set in 10/13pt Linotron Bembo
Typeset by Cambrian Typesetters, Frimley
Colour origination by Fotographics, Hong Kong
Printed and bound in the UK by Richard Clay, Bungay

A catalogue record for this book is available
from the British Library.

ISBN 1 85283 124 3

CONTENTS

ACKNOWLEDGEMENTS

NO angling writer can produce a book without considerable help from others. Allow me therefore to thank the editing and design team; the mates who leave their own fishing to photograph me; and a very special thank you to good friend Dave Batten who has made such a fine job of the line drawings.

John Wilson
Great Witchingham
1991

INTRODUCTION

WINTER and summer, whether you are knee deep in snow or wading the cool shallows amongst beds of streamer weed, the chub is always available. It is the utility fish of freshwater, forever willing to grab the bait when other species are not.

It is the choice of those winter fishermen who are not concerned about pike fishing. It is unfortunately despised by the trout fisherman who, having paid more for his chalkstream spot than the deposit on a new Porsche, unhooks the ghastly chub with total contempt. But the chub doesn't care.

Once over the magical 5 lb mark it becomes one of the richest prizes in freshwater fishing. In real terms it is far more of a catch than a 20 lb carp or pike. Yet fish of less than half this specimen size are the wonder of small boys, and without question the saviours of match fishing. In their adult form chub are more than strong enough to be continually caught, retained, weighed and returned until caught again. They are durable, always a strong subject and fun to photograph, and they are there for everyone to enjoy.

My difficulty in writing about chub has been to keep within the bounds of the allocated word count, to decide not what to put in, but very much what can honestly be left out. This, perhaps best of all, sums up the species that offers more diverse sport than any other two species combined.

Naturally this book contains my favourite methods for catching chub, which are in no way the whole story. More so than with any other species, we are forever learning the trade.

CHAPTER ONE

THE
SPECIES

CHUB
(Leuciscus cephalus)

Only occasionally is the chub mistaken for other indigenous freshwater species. Immature chub can be confused with and thus mistaken for large dace, although even the mouth of a small chub is unusually large, while both its dorsal and anal fins are convex (rounded), as opposed to those of the dace (and roach) which are concave and circle inwards along the outside edge.

When adult there is little to confuse the chub with any other British freshwater species, but one fish guaranteed to make you look more than twice because it looks so incredibly similar is the Asiatic grass carp now being purposefully stocked into southern carp waters. During the 1980s grass carp were accidentally introduced via the Anglian Water Authority's fish farm at Hellesdon, near Norwich, into the nearby River Wensum. From there odd specimens have even spread into the Yare and Waveney. And whenever the odd 8 or 9 lb grass carp turns up, the captor imagines he has broken the chub record until verification proves otherwise. Actually, grass carp cannot reproduce in our climate so the existence of these 'river' grass carp is very much a finite one.

However, whenever chub and grass carp exist together in stillwaters it takes an experienced eye to be sure of differentiating between them beneath the surface. I can remember, in the 1970s, when the Ministry of Agriculture and Fisheries experimentally stocked young grass carp into the moat surrounding Oxborough Hall near Downham Market in west Norfolk. They quickly grew and once mature their presence fooled many an experienced specimen hunter who, upon apparently seeing dozens of record chub from 8 lb to over 12 lb swimming around beneath the ducks and slurping down bread crusts with equal abandon, thought they had truly struck gold.

Two immediate differences between chub and grassies, when viewed head on, are the latter's smaller mullet-shaped mouth and its eyes, which are extremely low set almost in the middle of its head. In addition, whilst chub tend to 'hover' horizontally, grassies do so at a distinct head-up angle. The grass carp's tail is also noticeably larger than that of the chub. But enough of the grass carp, fine fighter though it is. Let's concentrate on our hero.

The chub is renowned for its broad, blunt, almost bullet-shaped head and truly cavernous mouth rimmed by thick, white, rubbery lips, old rubber lips being just one of its numerous nicknames. It is ungraciously called 'skelly' or 'scalies' in Scotland by game fishermen, who see little merit in its greedy habits when it has the audacity to take their fly intended for much higher forms of life, namely trout and salmon. And it is called Chevin (a lovely term) by ardent chub enthusiasts.

At the rear of its throat, buried in soft tissue as with all cyprinids, the chub has a formidable pair of pharyngeal teeth, each with a double row of hooked crushers. These are incredibly powerful and are used by the chub for mincing up its food to pulp prior to swallowing. Hard-shelled crustaceans such as the crayfish, and the meaty flesh of other small fishes, are all gulped back and given the crushing treatment. Never put your finger down a chub's throat to dislodge the hook, as it will emerge looking and feeling as though it has been smashed beneath the head of a 3 lb hammer.

Body coloration often depends upon water colour and temperature. While the back is usually a dark grey, the flanks can vary from a distinct brassiness in the summer, to pale silver in the colder water of winter. The dorsal fin and tail are painted a dark blueish grey. The pectoral fins appear translucent with little more than a light grey tint, and the flanks blend into a belly of creamy white.

Chub from clear flowing rivers are always more vividly and intensely coloured than those living in permanently coloured water, while stillwater chub are noticeably more darkly painted.

Isaac Walton credited the chub with being the most fearful of fish, which of course is perfectly true. Learn to creep up upon a chub basking in a small clear-watered stream without its having an inkling of your presence, and you are almost there. Chub are nowhere near so difficult to tempt provided they have not been scared first. Clear-water chub, especially, seem to possess eyes in their tails and are particularly unforgiving of the slightest unnatural bankside vibrations or the sudden appearance of a silhouette against the skyline which should not be there. And being a shoal fish, the fears of one are instantly transmitted to the others. The maximum length for the species is around 24 to 25 in, though most adult chub vary between 16 and 20 in, depending upon the richness of the environment in which they live. For instance, those competing in a shoal of 20 to 50 other chub, in a river that is densely populated with competition species as well as other chub shoals, may never exceed 2 to 3 lb in weight. Yet put that same chub (from an early age when growth potential is unlimited) into a rich environment low in fish stocks, and ultimately it may grow to exceed 5 lb in weight, perhaps even more.

Even mature chub averaging 3 to 4 lb transferred from a fertile river to a stillwater where there is less competition will show a significant, even considerable, weight increase in individual fish, far surpassing the ultimate weight they would have attained in the river.

I monitored the existence for several years of a dozen or so chub taken from the River Wensum and stocked into a small gravel pit that was already quite heavily stocked with carp of all shapes and sizes, where you might assume the carp would eat them out of house and home – but not so. Being opportunist feeders, those chub grew fat and wide across the shoulders on the hordes of stunted rudd and roach in the pit; within a few years most had grown to 5 lb plus, with two individuals weighing a shade over 6 lb. There is no way those same chub, had they been left to compete with countless others in the River Wensum, would all have attained anywhere near the same weight increase – one or two perhaps, but certainly not all of them.

Because chub do not breed successfully in stillwater fisheries (unless a stream flows through it) perhaps, instead, they utilize all their energies in amassing a greater body size. Or is it that they simply expend less energy by not having to face and work against a strong flow. As a rule any species in a stillwater will ultimately grow to a far larger size than their running-water counterparts. And if ever a chub is caught topping that magical 10 lb barrier, I will wager that a stillwater fishery produces it. As it is, chub of between 7 and 8 lb are around the accepted optimum size likely to come from either still or running water.

CHAPTER TWO

ABOUT CHUB

FEEDING

Make no mistake about it, the chub is amongst the greediest of our freshwater fish. It may even be more of a glutton than the carp, which is the reason why, almost regardless of water temperature and conditions, you can usually find a chub or two willing to suck in your bait. Its reputation for having a catholic taste towards food is an understatement. In fact, I cannot think of a single known freshwater bait that the chub will not eat or a technique by which it cannot be caught.

It feeds upon all available aquatic insect life, including the larger nasties such as the ditiscus beetle and dragonfly larvae, and the entire crustacean family from the lowly shrimps and snails to the freshwater crayfish, whose armour-plating is quickly smashed by the chub's powerful pharyngeal teeth. Chub will consume newts, frogs, toads and the tadpoles of each, and small fishes of every species including their own.

Although they thrive in stillwaters when stocked, chub are river fish first and foremost. They make full use of everything the river provides, from the mish-mash of titbits continually brought down by the current, to fry shoals hugging the shallows, and into which they can often be seen lungeing during the summer months. Chub love minnows, bleak and gudgeon, young dace, bream, chub and roach, and even baby eels. Young lampries are considered even more of a delicacy.

Other fish do at times make up a large part of the chub's daily diet, and from a very early age. Chub of just 4 to 5 in long, for instance, feed on tiny fry, and can pose a nuisance to trout fishermen, who regularly hook them on large, gaudy patterns representative of fish fry. Do not be fooled by the fact that chub in hard-fished, clear rivers can suck in

At the back of the chub's throat are those impressive pharyngeal teeth. They are capable of crushing any small fish, and even the hard shell of the freshwater crayfish, to a pulp for easy swallowing.

a single caster and blow out the case without moving the float. A 3 lb chub can gobble up a 5 in roach, convert it to minced fish and swallow it in less time than it takes a pike to do the same. And a really big chub, say 5 lb and more, easily has the capacity and equipment for dealing with round-bodied fish like dace of up to ½ lb.

Paradoxically, chub also eat a certain quantity of vegetation, blanket weed especially – perhaps for the shrimps, nymphs, or minute molluscs it contains, perhaps simply because they like it. Wild fruits are also popular with chub, blackberries, hawthorns and particularly elder-berries which fall into the water during windy weather providing them with a juicy seasonal feast. There is no mystery in the fact that large, overhanging elder trees invariably produce the best sport of all on the river. Chub also rapidly discover a liking for particles intended for attracting barbel into the swim. Those pre-baited with stewed hempseed and hook baits, samples of mini boilies, luncheon-meat cubes, sweetcorn, casters, peanuts and so on (in fact, any particle and any boilie), invariably fill up with chub long before barbel.

However, it is a nice problem and one the chub

fisherman should remember. Small wonder that shoals of good, average-sized chub dominate river systems once they get a strong hold – often at the expense of the roach. I have fished numerous rivers over the past 30 years that once were fabulous roach fisheries and contained either few or no chub at all, but which are now far more prolific in chub than roach. The upper reaches of my local river Wensum, for instance, is a prime example. The chub quite

Most adult chub vary between 10 and 20 in long, and weigh somewhere between 2 and 4 lb.

simply is a more aggressive and efficient eating machine, and is just about the perfect angler's fish. You can catch it long trotting, laying on, freelining, ledgering, spinning, on surface plugs, wobbling deadbaits or livebaits, and with a fly rod using both wet and dry flies or small artificial lures. It will suck in crusts from the surface, a dead fish off the bottom, or grab a lure being trolled behind a boat. And if I have left anything off this list, I am sure the chub would willingly oblige.

During the winter months, like all cyprinids, the chub's metabolism drastically slows down and it requires a much smaller intake of food on a much less frequent basis. Quite simply, the colder the water becomes, fewer are the chances of chub becoming ravenous. In the most severe weather, when the river's surface is partly frozen over, it will nevertheless still continue to feed long after roach and bream have shut off. And though it may take several minutes to approach a small piece of flake ledgered static on the bottom when water temperature is little above freezing, I cannot remember not being able to induce at least a few tentative knocks. Whenever sub-zero weather sets in along my local Wensum valley, fields covered in snow, the river a cold grey unwelcoming colour, I am forever grateful to the chub for providing me with some sport.

REPRODUCTION

Chub are usually the next coarse species to spawn after pike, perch and dace, although a long, really chilly spring may still find the females pot-bellied at the end of June. I have in fact seen chub spawning as early as the middle of April and as late as the first week in July.

Always the shoals congregate in the fastest shallows, usually over a gravel and weedy bottom. Like the cyprinids, the males are distinguishable from the females by the white spawning tubercles which appear on their foreheads. These rough nodules are used for butting the females and to stimulate the release of the eggs, which are immediately sprayed with the white milt of the male as they fall to the bottom, adhering to stones and plants. If the water temperature remains constant, the fry will emerge within 10 days. They will feed initially on minute algae and planktons until they are large enough to manage aquatic insects and small, bottom-dwelling crustaceans. This is followed in part (for the rest of their lives) by an animal diet. Thus they become predatory at an extremely early age.

Concentrations of chub massing on the shallows during the close season as an early grouping process prior to the spawning is not only a sight to behold, but also to be studied. For those interested in catching really large chub, or at the least in ascertaining to just what size the chub in a particular stretch actually reach, there is no more accurate formula than keeping a close eye on the stream or river through polaroid glasses through late April and May. During this time chub from every conceivable hole and hideout far downstream migrate up river into ridiculously fast bubbly water – exactly the kind of shallows you would not normally fish, where for most of the year you expect only to find minnows.

The true bulk and length of certain fish can then clearly be seen, but remember that within a few weeks all will be repositioned back downstream again in their respective habitats after completing propagation of the species. So there will be much searching ahead. You will, however, have gained a clear idea as to whether a particular stretch holds chub of the size you seek.

As they need running water to stimulate the urge to reproduce, chub living in stillwaters do not usually even try to spawn. Only in lakes, reservoirs and pits into which water flows, therefore, can you expect to see chub gathering on the shallows during the spring.

DISTRIBUTION

Chub are found throughout most of the large river systems of Europe, particularly in the middle and lower reaches, as indeed they are throughout most river systems in England except for Devon and Cornwall. They live only in the most southern of Scottish rivers and while rivers like the Anan breed chub of huge proportions, their presence is

Although the chub's metabolic rate slows down during the winter months it nevertheless continues to feed, providing consistent sport in the smallest stream, such as this backwater of Berkshire's River Kennet.

barely tolerated by salmon and seatrout anglers. They have only limited distribution in Wales, although the mighty River Wye is arguably the most prolific chub fishery within the British Isles.

Chub find their way into gravel pits, reservoirs and lakes adjacent to many rivers either by following the course of feeder streams and inlets or across flooded meadows during periods of high spate. A good friend who for a part-living catches eels with fyke nets from along the River Wensum valley told me the ultimate, but perfectly true, fishy tale epitimizing just how far chub will travel during floods.

In a rip-roaring full spate when the Wensum had breached both banks, the water rose above the channels beneath a local road bridge and spewed onto either side of the brickwork across the road to a depth of a good 2 ft. It was quite mild at the time and, as all netsmen are aware, eels are most likely to be running during such circumstances. Just before dark Roger actually set his fyke nets (the road was closed to traffic all week) stretching down the road across which the main flow had been diverted. In the morning he was flabbergasted, when lifting the nets, to see what he had caught: among the eels were over 20 chub to close on 4 lb.

Only in recent years has the chub's worth as an ideal, controllable stock fish for selected stillwaters been fully realized. It grows large, while at the same time helping to control shoals of stunted nuisance fish, without competing for the same food source as say tench, carp or bream. For this reason, more and more stillwater fisheries are now being stocked with limited numbers of chub.

Chub are among the most common river species, particularly in the middle and lower reaches. And in the rich, clear-flowing weedy waters of the famous Royalty fishery on the Hampshire Avon they reach monstrous proportions.

CHAPTER THREE

LOCATING CHUB IN RIVERS AND STREAMS

SUMMER

Find any sort of cover in freshwater, be the river a mere stream or a wide tidal channel, and you will have located a potential chub swim (fig. 1). Although chub do shoal up in open midstream swims in both deep and shallow rivers whether weed-beds are present or not, they much prefer, and are more likely to be found, wherever there is access to cover above their heads. So let us consider the numerous habitats chub are likely to use as both home and refuge.

But first a word of advice for summer location, when most rivers run reasonably clear and when future sport relies upon visual proof, and your ability to spot the chub before it or they see you. Do not under any circumstances leave home without polaroid glasses. Forget the bait by all means, because natural baits can easily be gathered from beside the river (see bait chapter), but make a point of including your polaroids above all else.

I much prefer those with bright yellow lenses, which not only eliminate reflective glare from the surface, but also provide increased visibility for the immediate surroundings both in and out of the water during low light values such as dusk and dawn. And these, of course, happen to be the best times for catching the chub off its guard, whether you are fishing or merely spotting. There is, however, a strong case for choosing polaroids with darker grey lenses for those rare occasions during bright sunshine in the middle of the day when chub are feeding ravenously.

during gales or because of old age, make sure you capitalize on the situation. Within days (sometimes hours) of a large tree crashing into the river, chub will take up residence. And it has been my experience that the largest trees will contain the largest concentrations of chub. Moreover, the snaggiest spot within the honeycomb of sub-surface passages created by the sunken woodwork invariably harbours the largest specimens. That there is a pecking order for occupying the choicest swims is beyond doubt.

Marginal plant cover

Marginal caverns formed beneath rafts of floating sweet reed grass (fig. 4), sedges, dense beds of watercress, and so on, have enormous capacity for hiding chub. It is along the banks of clear-flowing rivers prolific in sweet reed grass that you can walk for mile upon mile fish-spotting for chub, and come to believe that there is next to nothing worth catching in the entire river. In fact, all the better, wiser fish are well out of sight beneath the first 2 to 6 ft of floating raft, most of which looks like part of the bank until you try walking on it. A 5 ft wide by 100 yd long raft

FIGURE 4 *Sweet reed grass*

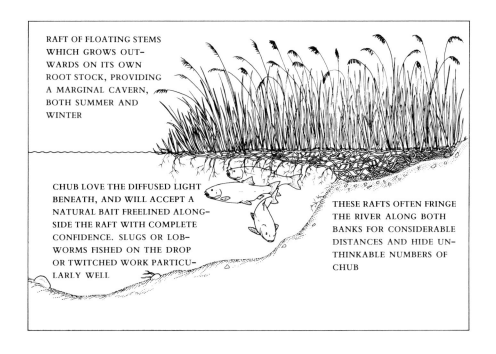

RAFT OF FLOATING STEMS WHICH GROWS OUT- WARDS ON ITS OWN ROOT STOCK, PROVIDING A MARGINAL CAVERN, BOTH SUMMER AND WINTER

CHUB LOVE THE DIFFUSED LIGHT BENEATH, AND WILL ACCEPT A NATURAL BAIT FREELINED ALONG- SIDE THE RAFT WITH COMPLETE CONFIDENCE. SLUGS OR LOB- WORMS FISHED ON THE DROP OR TWITCHED WORK PARTICU- LARLY WELL

THESE RAFTS OFTEN FRINGE THE RIVER ALONG BOTH BANKS FOR CONSIDERABLE DISTANCES AND HIDE UN- THINKABLE NUMBERS OF CHUB

It is no coincidence
that big chub prefer
the sanctuary provided
by the tangled roots
and branches of fallen
trees. Nevertheless,
they are catchable
from these spots by
anglers who are
willing to try hit-and-
haul tactics.

Chub love to retreat
behind overhanging
marginal plants such
as watercress, sweet
reed grass, rushes, and
even the beautiful
Himalayan Balsam,
from which Charlie
Clay winkled this
modest fish despite the
bright sunshine.

Despite a complete lack of marginal cover, Bruce Vaughan crawls into a casting position that allows him to flip a freelined worm across to the opposite bank and whack into a fine chub.

of floating sweet reed grass can obscure a very large number of chub.

Unfortunately, this particular plant can drastically narrow a river due to the sediment which gathers around its enormous root structure and which eventually is claimed back by the land. It does, however, tend to keep whatever channel is left to a reasonably uniform depth, often with as much water below the leading edges as there is in mid-stream: a good point to remember for both summer and winter fishing.

Though the careless angler who walks heavily on marshy ground will rarely see chub as they slide out from beneath overhangs to move up river and feed, it is the mixture of diffused light and tranquillity which makes the chub feel safe beneath overhanging vegetation. During

undisturbed daylight hours chub love nothing better than
to lie facing the flow on the very edge of the overhang, or
even a few inches beyond the trailing edges in clear water,
on the look out for titbits brought downstream by the
current or food dropping into the water from the land.
However, they can melt away very quickly.

I remember having this illustrated many years back
when, as a teenager, I stalked chub on the River Rib in
Hertfordshire. After taking several minutes to crawl on all
fours along a high, exposed bank and slither down to blend
into the surroundings behind a clump of tall reeds, my
patience and stealth were rewarded by seeing four chub
facing the current immediately upstream from a floating
patch of watercress, completely unaware of my presence.
It was a case of which one would take the bait first, and
that is how easy chub fishing during the summer months
can be for those willing to wear drab clothes and move
stealthily whilst keeping low to the water. However, quite
suddenly the four chub quickly turned tail just as the
freelined slug was in mid flight, and by the time it landed
on the surface they had vanished from sight as though
scared by my casting. Was the glint of the sun's rays
reflecting off the line? Did my watch-face catch the sun just
at the wrong moment and warn them? No, it was neither.
A good 10 seconds or so after they had disappeared my
ears picked up the crunching noise of rubber boots. This
was soon followed by a fellow angler, one of the 'had any
luck mate' brigade, with not the slightest clue about chub
fishing in little rivers. He stood bolt upright, laden down
with mega-basket and rod holdall, sporting a shirt so white
that only a soap-powder manufacturer would be proud.

I may well have missed out on catching one of the four
chub that day, but the experience taught me a valuable
lesson about how sensitive the species is to bankside
vibrations. Locate the chub without it being aware of your
presence and it can even prove easy to catch. Locate it and
subsequently scare it, and at the very least you will need to
chase after it with ultra-light tackle (upon which it could be
lost) just in order to tempt a bite.

With regard to chub hiding behind marginal plant cover,
expect the presence of a fish, during the summer months at
least, under the smallest of floating canopies which hang
out over the water, and so creep stealthily at all times.

Bullrushes

Owing to its preference for clear-flowing, well-oxygenated pure water and a hard gravel bottom, the bullrush (not to be confused with the reedmace, which sports those distinctive cigar-like seed-heads) is nowhere near so common in British rivers as it once was. But wherever it exists in large beds that sprout from the gravel, whether along marginal shallows or in the middle of the river, you can expect numbers of chub. They love especially to occupy small clearings between thick clumps of rushes, and can often be seen holding station just out of the main flow, waiting for food to be brought to them.

The bullrush has incredibly tough, round, dark green tapering, onion-like stems in which chub soon find sanctuary unless you prize them out quickly on suitable tackle. A 5 or 6 lb line is none too heavy for extracting even modest-sized chub quickly from bullrushes. And whenever specimens, say fish of 4 lb upwards, are expected do not be afraid of stepping up your tackle accordingly. A 7 or 8 lb line, for instance, would perhaps not seem particularly sporting for catching a 4 to 5 lb chub, but neither is a hook left in that fish trailing several feet of line.

Long, flowing weedbeds

I use the word 'weed' here only as a rough description because plants like the water crowfoot, of which there are several varieties, with their delicate daisy-like flowers, are amongst the most beautiful of flowering aquatic plants. The potomogeton pondweeds also grow in long, flowing beds, providing a mass of tough, bright green leaves, beneath and between which chub love to hide throughout the summer months. So do not immediately discount distinctly open parts of the river barren of obvious bankside habitat features like overhanging trees. Down there close to the gravel bottom, beneath the mountain of greenery, in a world of silence and much reduced light, even on the brightest day, you can find chub, often in the kind of numbers you would consider absolutely impossible

On this very fast, weedy stretch of the Hampshire Avon John had to don chest-waders during the filming of his TV series, Go Fishing, *in order to extract the chub hooked on free-lined meat cubes, from between the long, flowing beds of rununculus.*

when viewing the same stretch of river from the bank through polaroid glasses.

Only in the early morning around dawn and again in the evening will chub choose to leave their habitat, rising to lie immediately below the surface to take advantage of hatching aquatic insect life.

Mill and weir pools

In turbulent mill and weir pools chub always feel happy about the extra depth of water above their heads, and the fact that the surface is broken by strong currents. To them it is as much sanctuary as the thickest weed-beds or submerged branches. Should the water flatten off during low levels, or the sluice be temporarily closed by the mill owner, the crafty chub will slink beneath the sill or work its way up into the pool under the mill house itself. Many old mills, whether still working or not, contain a dark cavernous sluice (completely hidden from view) into which water tumbles from above the mill in order to work the machinery. This is sometimes referred to as the

'turbine pit'. The largest chub of all are attracted to such mysterious sluices, which explains those rare one-off captures of giant chub, the size of which few anglers believe, quite simply because they are so rarely seen in the river proper. The goliath chub, of course, has been there all along. Hidden from view and leading a sedentary life during daylight hours, it only ventures into the open river under the cloak of darkness.

Observation and a stealthy approach, keeping down low to the water, are tactics demanded by small-stream chubbing in order to catch fish at close range.

Road and rail bridges

Despite the thoroughness and expertise of civil engineers, the power of flowing water is easily underestimated, which is why cavernous undercuts are created under ancient road and rail bridges. These are scoured to the chub's liking directly beneath the stantions. Depending on the support construction, whether reinforced concrete pillars, brick piers or piled columns, somewhere in a dark cavern you can be sure chub will be in residence.

Even without caverns, the darkness beneath large, wide road bridges can attract equally large concentrations of chub. Bridges over the Thames or Great Ouse, for instance, tend to be very prolific, with 30 to 40 fish to a shoal nothing out of the ordinary. A single-lane span crossing a countryside stream, on the other hand, will perhaps only have sufficient room to house a single chub or two. Only large brown trout ever seem to compete with chub for bridge habitats, though wherever they co-exist in real numbers, barbel are most likely to share with the chub, as is the odd group of specimen perch.

Canoe observation

Strange though it may seem, like most species chub are far less intimidated by someone's presence actually in or on the water than by that same person crunching along the bank. So if you own a canoe, put it to good use during the close season and during the middle of summer when levels are low and the water is crystal clear. Be careful, of course, not to upset other river fishermen by paddling through their swims.

Searching a river course by canoe is the most accurate method of location I know next to scuba-diving, and is by far the quickest way of ascertaining the whereabouts and numbers of chub in a previously unexplored part of the river. Providing you sit quietly with minimal paddle movement, chub will permit the canoe to come quite close before moving position.

Extremely long sections of the river, and even entire stretches between mills several miles apart, can be covered in a comparatively short space of time with the help of a fellow chub fisherman, two roof racks and a double canoe. The secret is to deposit one car at the downstream mill, before driving the canoe to the starting point well up river, where the second car is left. You can then go happily with the flow, allowing the current to drift the canoe close by all the obvious habitat swims, knowing transport is waiting for you at the other end. It is then a simple matter to pick up the second car.

In this way I have enjoyed many years of researching countless miles of the weedy, clear-flowing upper reaches of Norfolk's best chub rivers. Rivers so overgrown throughout much of their length that bankside observation is almost impossible, and at best is extremely arduous during the summer months.

Once a general outline of the river's potential has been obtained, I then set about more detailed exploration of all the choice spots seen from the canoe in a fish-as-I-go bankside wander. Swims too remote or completely inaccessible to be tackled from *terra firma* are mentally marked down, possibly to be fished at some time in the future from the canoe itself.

WINTER

Finding chub in winter with the rivers cold, running fast and often heavily coloured, is not so daunting as it would first appear. It is to a large extent merely a natural progression from summer chubbing. And it is just reward for the countless hours spent spotting and becoming familiar with the river's character when it was running clear, when the deeps and shallows, snags and clear runs,

FIGURE 5 *Winter chub*

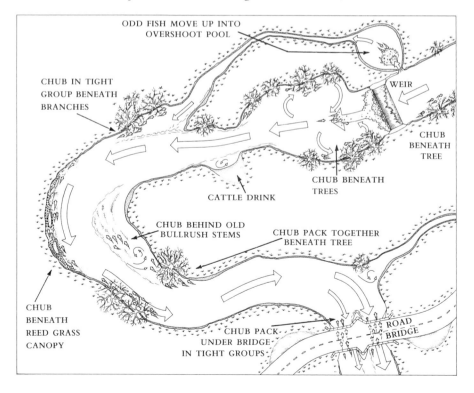

ODD FISH MOVE UP INTO OVERSHOOT POOL

CHUB IN TIGHT GROUP BENEATH BRANCHES

WEIR

CHUB BENEATH TREE

CHUB BENEATH TREES

CATTLE DRINK

CHUB BEHIND OLD BULLRUSH STEMS

CHUB PACK TOGETHER BENEATH TREE

CHUB BENEATH REED GRASS CANOPY

CHUB PACK UNDER BRIDGE IN TIGHT GROUPS

ROAD BRIDGE

weed-beds and gravel bars were all plainly visible. Therefore those who have done their homework and studied the
river exhaustively will know exactly where to look. They
will find that most of the choice 'feature' swims which held
chub during the summer will also produce throughout the
the coldest months (fig. 5).

Certain swims

Swims beneath road bridges, mill and weir pools, trees
overhanging acute bends, dense lines of trees, expecially
those whose trailing lower branches collect rafts of
flotsam, rotting weed, reed stems and the like: these are the
absolute certain winter chub haunts. They in fact contain
far greater numbers of fish when temperatures are low and
the shelter of summer weed throughout the river has been
killed off by heavy frosts and dissipated by flood water.

It stands to reason that chub which were spread
throughout the shallow runs both up and downstream of
feature swims only a few months back will not now wish
to feel vulnerable. They fall back or move up and pack into

*When conditions are
perfect – the river
coloured and dropping
slowly following a full
flood – big hauls of
chub are on the cards,
even from relatively
small rivers like
John's local Wensum.*

the nearest sizeable feature in which they feel comfortable.

Where trees are sparse, a single large overhanging willow might provide protection for a disproportionately large population of chub, certainly enough to keep you busy all day, whereas in the summer that same tree might shelter just a quartet of chub and warrant merely a couple of casts before moving on. And this is what I particularly like about winter chub fishing. Certain swims, even in small to medium-sized rivers, provide the opportunity of sitting there for most of the day and catching a bag of fish.

Most stretches of my local River Wensum above Norwich, for instance, are quite narrow even as chub rivers go. They seldom have more depth in the feature swims than 4 to 5 ft, yet bags of up to a dozen quality chub at a sitting are possible during the winter from any number of spots. And when conditions are perfect, which on the Wensum means a dropping river after heavy flooding coinciding with a spell of really mild weather, I have occasionally taken over 20 fish at one spot from the most productive swims. It is fair to say, however, that not all large concentrations of chub spend the winter in the sanctuary of perfect, picturebook feature swims.

Deep runs

Deep runs alongside thick beds of tall reeds or rushes, now brown and matted, or where the banking is almost vertical and reaches high above the water, are also much favoured by chub for winter quarters, particularly on the outside of wide or acute bends.

Deep gullies in the middle of generally shallow stretches should also not be overlooked, particularly where more obvious features do not exist. After all, those chub haven't jumped out on the bank or swum to another river. Despite the water looking grey, cold and unwelcoming, they will be lying somewhere, and finding them is all part of the fun.

Think of winter chubbing as a giant jigsaw puzzle based upon knowledge gained from observation at the waterside during the earlier part of the season, linked of course to any past experiences on the same river during colder weather. Unless heavy and prolonged flooding switches contours around, deep runs which produced chub during past winters should continue to do so.

Bullrushes

It pays to remember exactly where those dense beds of
bullrushes were situated during the summer (sometimes
the brown tops of a few stalks can be seen wavering just
above the surface), because down below, the remaining
roots and stalks help to create a natural barrier against even
the strongest currents, behind which chub love to hide.
Study the surface currents and see how tiny vortexes of
water spiral up after hitting the submerged bed of rotting
stalks, in order to pinpoint their exact position. And try to
picture in your mind the area of slack water created
immediately downstream, indicated by the water surface
above it becoming flat and smooth.

Sweet reed grass

Those thick, marginal beds of sweet reed grass (often
simply called rushes), beneath whose floating canopy chub
loved to hide during the brightness of a summer's day, also
provide winter quarters. The floating raft of matted brown
stems, decidedly spongey to walk beside, may not reach as
far into the river as in summer, but chub in good numbers
will be in residence. Study the marginal vegetation well
and look for sections on the outside of a bend, where the
current steadies as the depth increases. These spots are
great chub swims, and if a reasonable depth continues on
around the bend blending into a long even paced glide, an
extremely large concentration of chub is more than a
possibility.

Current direction

Small deviations in surface currents may not at first be
distinct, but the more you study current direction and
surface displacement, the more obvious it all becomes.
During the winter months, for instance, when the level is
up and the water coloured, large areas of very shallow
water unlikely to hold chub (except in full flood) are not
immediately apparent to those unfamiliar with the river.

Those who know it well don't bother with these barren swims, because they remember how the river was during the summer. And those who observe surface currents wherever they fish will, from the action of surface displacements, be able to distinguish between shallows and deeps. Remember how tiny vortexes of water are sent upwards when hitting the dying stalks of bullrushes sprouting from the gravel shallows. The same spiralling and displacement occurs when fast currents hit the tiniest of pebbles. Thus gravel shallows are easily depicted on the surface by completely 'broken' water, despite the fact that through heavily coloured water the bottom cannot be seen.

Having said all this, for part of the day chub may very well choose to occupy the fastest, shallowest part of the swim, but over a 24-hour period their requirements are consistent. They prefer to hold station in a quiet slack out of the main current force, but not so far away that they cannot nip out every so often and suck in a juicy titbit. Maximum food for minimum effort aptly sums up the chub's outlook towards life. Of course in mild winter conditions chub are renowned for being continually on the move, and will follow a food source (the angler's loose feed) from a considerable way downstream. But in the coldest, sub-zero weather and freezing winds the shoal will huddle together, loathe to move very far. And when you decide to fish in these conditions, pinpoint accuracy is essential for success.

Low temperatures

Much depends on the daytime temperature and whether it increases a few degrees or not. On some days, chub might move several yards to a bait when the light values increase at around midday. On another day, they will not budge an inch until dusk sets in. And then one solitary knock on the quiver tip is all you will get.

On a very cold river the bait may need to land on their noses for bites to materialize. Let me recall a particular outing to illustrate the point, not for the couple of 3 lb chub it produced but because it was nice to put the jigsaw together in just a couple of hours's fishing, when the entire

Observation of the directions of surface currents will help you pinpoint the position of winter chub. Look how the flow is deflected across the river by the fence in the foreground, providing a long, tempting slack behind it.

Wensum valley lay 6 in deep in snow. Upon arriving at the river near Taverham, I stood with eyes fixed upon the steel grey water. The surface looked angry as well as cold, and very fast. Patterned by a thousand separate tiny vortexes, the river (running right to left) splayed out around an acute bend, hitting the high bank where I stood (fig. 6). Where would the chub be hiding, bellies touching bottom and heads down? Under the bank? No, the current changed direction far too much and they would want to hold station against a steady flow. Nor were they on the opposite bank, where only inches of water existed above a massive bed of silt deposited by the slow back-eddy. With the Wensum high, however, a newcomer to the valley might well be fooled by such a superb-looking swim.

In the middle of the river just downstream of the bend a multitude of little swirls spewed up from the bottom, pinpointing the stubble remains of the previous summer's bullrush clumps. A few yards downstream these surface swirls evened out for little more than a couple of yards; a strip of surface water no wider or longer than a household bath tub, and it was exactly what I was looking for. The surface then broke up again as the bottom shelved up on to

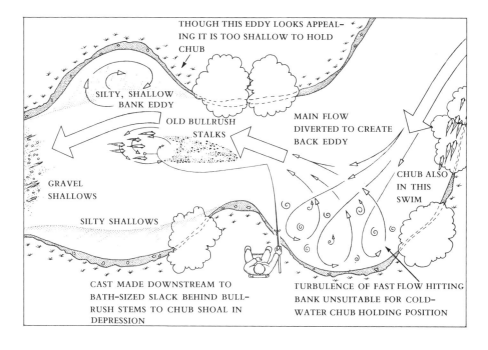

THOUGH THIS EDDY LOOKS APPEAL-
ING IT IS TOO SHALLOW TO HOLD
CHUB

SILTY, SHALLOW
BANK EDDY

OLD BULLRUSH
STALKS

MAIN FLOW
DIVERTED TO CREATE
BACK EDDY

GRAVEL
SHALLOWS

CHUB ALSO
IN THIS
SWIM

SILTY SHALLOWS

CAST MADE DOWNSTREAM TO
BATH-SIZED SLACK BEHIND BULL-
RUSH STEMS TO CHUB SHOAL IN
DEPRESSION

TURBULENCE OF FAST FLOW HITTING
BANK UNSUITABLE FOR COLD-
WATER CHUB HOLDING POSITION

FIGURE 6 *Under-
standing current
patterns for chubbing
in cold water*

*Pinpoint accuracy
when placing the bait
is essential when
ledgering for chub in
sub-zero conditions.
Kevin Gardner from
Norwich was obvi-
ously on the ball to
tempt this fine River
Yare 4-pounder.*

gravel shallows, where massive beds of water crowfoot clog the surface throughout the summer months. To the river fisherman, chub were in that small stretch of water.

On quiver-tipped bread flake, after introducing a few small balls of mashed bread, came four hittable bites. Each took several minutes to materialize once the bait had settled on the bottom. Fingers and ears were very cold. There was ice in the tiny rings on the end of the quiver tip, and finally there were two chub in the net. The only proof that an angler had been silly enough to explore the Wensum that cold day was the Yeti-like footprints of my thermal boots.

FLOODED RIVERS

As anglers are only too aware, brooks, streams and even large rivers can become quite unrecognizable following weeks of heavy rain or snow. So again, prior knowledge of all the existing features helps enormously towards locating

FIGURE 7 *Flooded river chub*

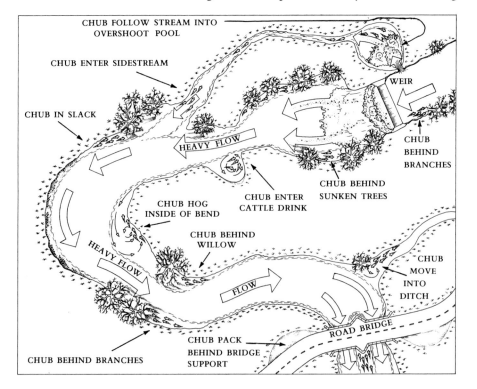

and subsequently extracting a few chub from situations which at first look to be hopeless (fig. 7).

Spots where ditches or side streams converge with the main flow, slacks behind large sunken willows, cow drinks, overshoot pools (stagnant during the summer), slacks immediately behind wide bridge supports, and so on: these are the natural hiding-places which chub seek out and quickly move into to avoid facing the full force and continual barrage of debris-laced flood waters.

In rivers absent of definite features, expect to find chub very close in – within inches of the bank immediately downstream of the bends, where current speed is noticeably that much slower. For example, swims which in the summer hold no more than a few inches of water or may even be completely dry, such as the baked sides of cow drinks.

LOCATING CHUB
IN STILLWATERS

Finding chub in large stillwaters is one of the hardest tasks of all, especially when you consider that only a small percentage of gravel pits, even among those adjacent to river systems, actually contain any chub at all. And those which do, rarely hold more than the occasional small group or shoal (see pp. 11 and 18). So ask around among other anglers and at your local specialist tackle shop, to find out exactly which pits, lakes or reservoirs are known for producing chub within the local area.

Armed with polaroid glasses and a pair of binoculars, the best time for visual location is during the summer. At this time lakes and pits are warm and clear, and the chub are patrolling as they do in formation, forever on the move, and swimming noticeably faster than would seem appropriate for a fish seeking food.

Having observed this peculiar behaviour, I am convinced it is something to do with the fact that by swimming fast they simulate the rush of water that would be passing across their gills in flowing water. Similarly, I have also regularly observed a group of several chub that spend the greater part of their time beneath a line of overhanging

Stillwater chub are attracted to the same kinds of hideout habitats as in flowing water. Overhanging trees and snaggy tangles are particularly favoured.

willows in the smaller of my own two lakes. Their particular forte during hot summer afternoons is to fan each other with their tails. They move slowly around each other, twisting and twining through the lapping branches with their tails gently splashing the surface.

Initially I took this for surface feeding upon aquatic insects. However, after spending many hours observing them through binoculars, I am of the opinion that these chub are encouraging well-oxygenated water to pass across each others' gills. As this ritual is only performed during the heat of the day, when dissolved oxygen in a small, overgrown pit is perhaps at its lowest, there would seem to be no other logical explanation.

This curiosity does rather sum up stillwater chub in one word: unpredictable. You never quite know where they will turn up next, or whether they will be inclined to feed. Once stocked into stillwaters, chub definitely alter in character and become even more suspicious than carp. Gone is that instant, unthinking aggression seen in a river chub as it rushes from a standing start to suck in a freelined crust or slug in case one of its shoal buddies gets there first. Stillwater chub are renowned for taking their time and

then refusing a bait. In small stillwaters full of character they certainly relate to the same kind of jungle swims which exist in rivers – such as over-hanging trees, sunken bushes and trees. However, in huge, featureless, wind-swept gravel pits lacking any obvious habitats, they become nomadic and possibly spend much of their time following the fry shoals. They do, however, respond to surface baits like floating crust and to surface-popping plugs. They also respond to regular pre-baiting along the margins with both bread and deadbaits (see pp. 116 and 120). The fact remains, however, that stillwater chub pose an exasperating proposition on the basis of their limited numbers alone. At best, you could well be trying to locate (with the possibility of catching just one or two of them) a group of just eight or nine fish in a lake or a gravel pit several acres in size. Nevertheless, they offer the ultimate freshwater challenge.

As I mentioned before, an enormous amount of recon-naissance work needs to be done on location before even considering a few sessions after stillwater chub, particularly during the winter months when, due to temperature alone, all species are noticeably less active.

When stocked into stillwaters full of small shoal fish, the predatory chub grows to huge proportions. John took this 6 lb 7 oz specimen on float-ing crust from a tiny, overgrown gravel pit during a February mild spell.

CHAPTER FOUR

TACKLE

AS chub can be caught on just about every natural and synthetic bait ever invented, plus all types of artificial lures from flies to spinners, and by every technique in the book, whatever tackle you own will suffice for catching them. To specialize, however, and to use gear specific to the technique you wish to enjoy, always provides greater pleasure. So starting with rods, let us consider the wide variety of tackle by which the chub may be taken.

RODS

Float rods

While most general-purpose glass and carbon rods of 11 ft plus will suffice, for laying on or stret pegging a slack close into the bank, or long trotting a float way downstream to spooky chub in clear water, the ideal tool for the float enthusiast is a three-piece 13 ft waggler rod. Many top rod manufacturers actually offer a choice of narrow-profile carbon fibre match-come-trotting rods in both stick-float and waggler actions. However, with its ultra-fine, spliced-in tip and fast action, the stick-float rod is a little too delicate for my liking for a fish that often has to be bullied upstream through quite strong flows. I much prefer the easier action and increased durability of the waggler rod, which, when necessary, can handle super-fine hook links in addition to reel lines of up to 4½ lb test. It is an extremely versatile tool indeed.

Some manufacturers still insist on putting ridiculously long handles on their float rods, which means that if the reel is fitted at the top of the handle where it is most functional, 6 in of extra handle protrudes from the elbow. This is not only a waste of money, but, in terms of line pick up, creates a shorter, less effective rod. Be particular in the tackle shop and reject rods with handles longer than 22–23 in, and those which are over-thick. Cork or composite handles between 7/8 and 1 in in diameter are fine.

Rod rings should be stand off and lined for reduced wear. Rods with unlined rings are cheaper to buy, but more expensive in the long run because after a couple of seasons hard use they will start to groove, and may cost you a big chub when the line shreds. The very lightest and strongest waggler rods are manufactured from a high-percentage carbon blank wrapped with a shock-absorbing strengthener such as 'kevlar'. Being narrow in profile and snappy in action, they cut easily through the air to hit tiny bites even at distance, yet will bend progressively in the upper sections to absorb the lunges of chub in a heavy flow, regardless of hook size.

Ledger/freelining rods

Without doubt, the best kind of rod for all-round ledger fishing in running water (and stillwaters for that matter) is the two-piece Avon with its progressive, all-through action. This is how big fish can be subdued in fast currents, because by bending all the way through (as opposed to just in the tip section) the rod does all the work and thus absorbs pressure on the line and hook length. So beware of rods bearing the Avon label that do not possess an all-through action, or you will be pulling the hook out or snapping the line on more chub than is healthy.

Most Avon rods have a test curve of around 1 1/4 lb. If you multiply this by 5 (the correct formula for ascertaining suitable line strengths), you will be able to pull into fish using straight ledgered or freelined baits with lines varying between 5 and 7 1/2 lb, and know that you are equipped with a matching outfit, with both line and rod 'stretching' together.

This is not to say that lighter lines cannot be used, however. Ledgering for chub in cold, clear water some-times dictates a reduction in hook size to a 16 or an 18, tied to 2 ft of 1 1/2–2 lb test merely to stimulate a few tiny bites. Reduced bite indication may not always show up on the basic rod tip, and this is where the Avon quiver tip rod comes into its own. With 20 in of solid glass tapered to a

bearing), smallish reel that has a roller in the bale arm (around which the line passes to reduce friction) and comes complete with two spools – one for fine lines, and a deeper spool capable of holding at least 100 yd of 6/7 lb test. It is also imperative that the reel has a smooth slipping clutch, so that on a pre-set drag setting line is freely taken by the chub, as opposed to it breaking. The choice between front drag adjustment on the spool itself or the more modern stern drag reels is a personal one.

I recommend a smallish model because slipping clutches are far more sensitive on these than on larger formats, and because lightweight compact reels are more in keeping with today's lightweight carbon rods.

Centre-pin reels

For many years now, in fact since my very early teens, I have preferred to use a centre-pin reel for float fishing. There is nothing to match that direct contact between a hooked chub and the line peeling from or being wound on to the drum.

When long-trotting for chub there is nothing like that direct feeling of contact provided by the centre-pin reel. This trio of River Waveney 4-pounders fell to a single caster on an 18 hook tied direct to 2 lb line.

Long-trotting enthusiasts who fancy switching from a closed face or fixed-spool reel over to the centre-pin can start at the more economical end of the scale by investing in one of the older secondhand models. Classics like the Trudex (my first centre-pin) Rapidex, Speedia or one of the fabulous Aerials originally made by Allcocks, are the reels to look out for, with the narrow-drum Match Aerial arguably the best of them all.

The Match Aerial is in fact currently being produced in small numbers through a specialist mail order service, after being unavailable for many years. It is a reel I love to use when chub fishing on the float, expecially with ultra-fine tackle. Another current centre-pin of quality is the Stanton Adcock, which runs superbly on ball bearings.

Baby multipliers

The choice of baby multipliers to match single-handed trigger-grip lure rods is, unfortunately, rather limited in the lower to medium price bracket. To be more precise, it is non-existent. You have to accept that to fully enjoy American-style casting, a suitable multiplier will cost twice as much as a quality fixed-spool reel. Having said this, I certainly would not wish to be without my collection, which includes trouble-free, magnetic casting-control models made by Ryobi, Daiwa and ABU. All are left-hand wind (the Ryobi is ambi-dextrous), which allows me to cast and play fish with my right hand, and perform the simple task of winding in with my left. All are fitted with automatic level wind, so necessary for foolproof casting and, though tiny, each of the spools can hold up to 200 yd of 8 lb test.

Fly reels

The requirements of a fly reel are considerably less than that of baby multipliers. All that is needed is a single-actioned reel with a ratchet, capable of holding 50 yd of backing beneath the fly line. This is not to prevent you from running out of line when a chub goes charging off downstream, but because well-filled fly reels ensure that the fly line has less 'memory' and peels off in large, limp coils. You need look no further than the British-made rimfly range made by Leeda. For lines 5 to 6 their lightweight model is ideal, while the regular '80' reel will accommodate a size 7 line plus backing admirably.

LINES

The reel lines I use for chub fishing vary between 2½ lb and 6 lb test (very occasionally 8 lb for working freelined baits and lures through snaggy swims), though lighter hook lengths down to a pound bottom are sometimes imperative for presenting tiny baits such as a single maggot or caster on a size 20 hook to educated chub in clear, snag-free water.

For trotting in medium-paced, snag-free rivers 2½ lb test reel line is ideal, whereas in heavy water such as the Hampshire Avon, where the chub average a good size, a 4½ lb reel line is none too light. When winter ledgering I prefer 5 lb test as a safety margin to take the wear and tear caused by continually lobbing out heavy leads or feeders. And during the summer when weed growth is prolific, again as a safety margin I may even step the reel line up to 6 lb, especially when freelining heavy natural baits into jungle-type swims which dictate a hit-and-hold tussle. I have an inherent distrust of narrow-diameter, low stretch, so-called revolutionary monofilament lines, much pre-ferring brands such as Bayer Perlon, Sylcast and Maxima, which contain sufficient elasticity to absorb the lunges of chub in fast currents or among thick weed-beds without fracturing.

HOOKS

For presenting baits like maggots or casters on hooks tied direct to the 2½ lb reel line, or on a finer hook length, I use spade-end hooks in sizes 16 to 22 because they look neater on the line. My favourite pattern is the Drennan forged carbon chub hook, which is more than strong enough even for quality-sized fish when hooked in open swims.

*A step down to small
hooks, light hook
lengths and a com-
pletely static bait, is
often the way of
putting chub on the
bank in extremely
clear, cold conditions.*

For size 14 hooks and larger I switch over to eyed hooks, and depend completely on the Drennan chemically-etched, round–bend, straight-eyed, carbon specimen hook. This model, while not over thick in the wire, has sufficient strength to cope with the largest chub without opening. The sizes I most regularly use are 10s to 4s tied direct on 4½ to 6 lb test. They accommodate most baits from a finger-nail sized piece of bread flake to large black slugs.

KNOTS

For tying spade-end hooks direct to the reel line or to a lighter hook length, use the easy spade-end knot (fig. 8A), which requires no threading or special tool. With this knot I can tie a size 20 spade end to a pound bottom behind my back with my eyes closed.

The best knot for eyed hooks is the mahseer knot in fig. 8B. It is easy to tie and faultless. With the neat eyes of modern, chemically-etched hooks, however, it is not always possible to pass the line twice through the eye. In which case, opt for the seven-turn tucked half blood knot shown in fig. 8C, remembering, as with all knots, to damp the line before gently pulling to tighten.

To join, say, 2 ft of fine hook length to the reel line for trotting with small hooks or for making a simple fixed

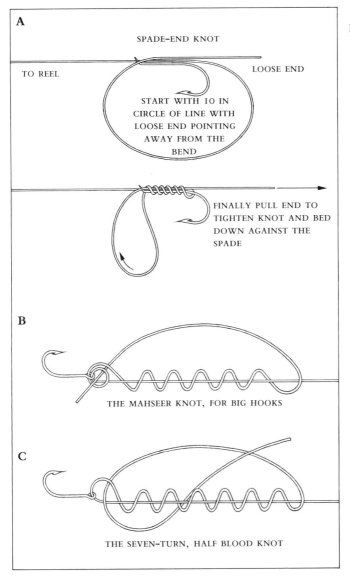

A

SPADE-END KNOT

TO REEL   LOOSE END

START WITH 10 IN
CIRCLE OF LINE WITH
LOOSE END POINTING
AWAY FROM THE
BEND

FINALLY PULL END TO
TIGHTEN KNOT AND BED
DOWN AGAINST THE
SPADE

B

THE MAHSEER KNOT, FOR BIG HOOKS

C

THE SEVEN-TURN, HALF BLOOD KNOT

FIGURE 8 *Knots 1*

paternoster, use the four-turn water knot shown in
fig. 9A. With this neat, reliable knot you can add a thicker
ledger or swimfeeder link to the reel line, which really does
stand away from the main line to alleviate tangle (fig. 9B),
or safely tie a lighter hook link to the heavier reel line
(fig. 9C).

Alternatively, a tiny size 12 swivel can be used as the
junction, as in fig. 9D. Don't forget to tie both reel line
and hook link to one end of the swivel and the ledger link

FIGURE 9 *Knots 2*

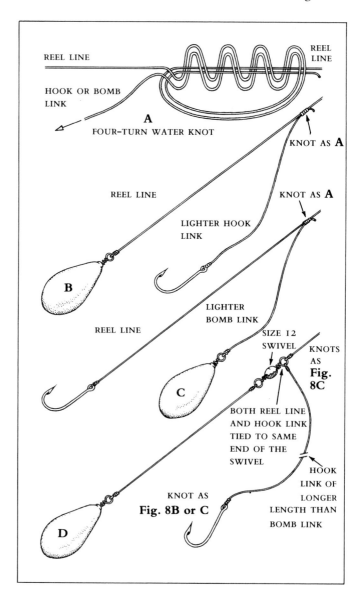

to the other, so that should the swivel fall apart your chub is still connected. If the swivel has a minute eye, use seven-turn tucked half blood knots.

You will no doubt have become aware that running ledger rigs are not mentioned, and that quite simply is because nowadays I do not use them. The fixed paternoster ledger is as effective, easier to construct and far less complicated. My reasons for using it exhaustively are explained in the ledgering chapter.

FLOATS

You will not require an armoury of different floats to catch chub. In fact, the vast majority of my fishing in running water is accomplished with just three popular patterns, plus a loaded carp-style controller (the ten-pin) for drifting down baits like bread crust.

Let us start with the most versatile float of all, the straight peacock waggler, which is fixed bottom end only, locked to the line with a large shot (usually the bulk shot) on either side, set ¼ in apart so it folds on the strike. I use a whole range of wagglers from 3 in to 12 in long and carrying from 2BB up to three swan shots. I use them for trotting swims more than two rod lengths out regardless of wind direction, in all slow to medium paced currents when using small hook baits. A silicone waggler float adaptor which locks on to the line (instead of the float) and into which the waggler's stem is pushed permits rapid change of floats.

In addition to trotting, I also use a waggler for laying on or stret pegging for chub, when it is attached to the line both top and bottom (see p. 109).

To present larger baits, and for combatting fast, often swirling currents, I use stumpy 'chubbers', which take from one to five swan shots and have a thick tip which can easily be seen when long trotted 20 or even 30 yd downstream. They are perfect for exploring distant runs in big, fast rivers. Attach this float both top and bottom with wide bands of silicone tubing to stop it slipping on the strike.

For the most delicate presentation in cold water using

Even specimen chub
fall to light float-
fishing techniques,
and the most versatile
float of all is the
straight peacock
waggler.

small hook baits you need a range of stick floats. These work well in conjunction with a flat calm or a gentle upstream wind, and like the chubber are attached top and bottom. The stick should be slightly overshotted so the tip is a mere blimp or dot on the surface and then held gently back as the bait trundles downstream wavering enticingly upwards every so often.

SUNDRIES

Landing-nets

When stalking chub during the summer along small rivers and streams heavily overgrown with dense, almost im-penetrable vegetation, there is nothing more infuriating than repeatedly having the mesh of a conventional landing-net catching up on the foliage. I prefer to use a folding

As few chub measure longer than 23–24 in, a 24 in round landing-net with a deep twin-mesh is just about the perfect tool for landing them.

trout net with a telescopic handle, which clips neatly out of harms way on a D-ring sewn to the back of my waistcoat. Mine has a lightweight, 20 in, rigid aluminium frame and is more than adequate for the largest chub. In fact, I sometimes use the same net when stalking carp in small overgrown fisheries, and have actually crammed a long, unexpected leather carp of 17¾ lb into the mesh. The only alteration has been to replace its standard, large (trout) mesh for a soft micro net, which turns it into the perfect landing-net for stalking chub.

For all other chub fishing, I use a 10 ft telescopic hollow glass pole, and a 24 in diameter round 'Wanderer' landing-net, which comes fitted with extra-deep minnow mesh sides so a big chub does not accidentally roll or jump out, and a soft, micro-mesh pan base.

To weigh your chub, do not bother with separate bags or weight slings. Unscrew the landing-net top from the pole and hook it on to the scales, remembering to deduct their weight afterwards. During high temperatures especially, this creates far less stress to the chub and the absolute minimum of physical harm because, as the landing-net is already wet, the fish's scales and body mucus will not be disturbed.

Keep-nets and sacks

Whenever wandering sessions involve a long walk from the car I never bother with carting keep nets along. A small, soft nylon keep-sack takes up minimal space in my camera bag and is always at hand should I catch a specimen worthy of a photo, early in the morning when light values are poor. The sack is pre-wetted and the chub left in the marginal shallows (beneath a bush) where it will lie quietly until later. Whilst wandering, however, I generally return each chub straight back into the swim as they are caught, and then move on.

Only when fishing the same swim for any length of time, when the chance of building up a very large bag is there, do I bother with a keep-net. To return numbers of fish to a swim from which you are trying to extract more is obviously not the best way of catching others from the same shoal, particularly in clear or low water conditions. In fact, there is no better way of inducing a premature end to the day's sport.

The best keep-nets are made from soft, knotless micro-mesh nylon. Some have two clips joining the last two rings, allowing the fish inside to be released through the bottom of the net, not tumbled down its full length. My advice is to purchase the longest you can afford.

CHAPTER FIVE

BAITS

DURING my early twenties I worked several months for a printing firm whose premises overlooked a pretty little stream that ran fast and shallow through beds of bright green watercress. In those days the stream (it was in fact a feeder stream to the nearby River Lea) contained numerous shoals of immature chub to around 1 lb that basked in the sunshine during summer afternoons directly beneath the print room in which letterpress machines banged noisily away. And those chub very soon learnt to accept a rather peculiar daily diet.

For a precious 30 minutes at lunchtime the machines were switched off, enabling the lads to nip across the road to the 'chippy'. I can vividly remember that first occasion when I flicked a hot chip into the stream. Its sudden arrival on the surface just upstream from the shoal sent a dozen or so chub absolutely crazy. A second chip was flicked in and disappeared with equal speed and another, and another, and so on. A new lunchtime activity was born, and soon everyone wanted to feed their fish and chips to those chub, which eagerly gobbled up anything and everything that was thrown in.

Why we gain such pleasure from feeding animals I am not sure, but we do. And when I left the printers, those chub were still supplementing their daily diet from the stream with fish and chips, sausage and chips, chicken and chips, or whatever.

The moral of this story is two-fold. It illustrates perfectly the fact that (unless you scare them) chub are unlikely to refuse anything edible which falls in their direction. And it proves to the fisherman that chub can be programmed, because within just a few days those chub were expecting their fish and chips at lunchtime. In short, pre-baiting is very worthwhile, whether it is just a few handfuls of hook bait scattered into the swim an hour before you actually fish or an organized pre-baiting plan executed over several days.

NATURAL BAITS FROM
THE RIVER

As I have mentioned already, there are numerous natural chub baits that can easily be obtained beside the river or actually in it. For this reason, it is always worth having a fine-mesh, rectangular aquarium net with you.

Bullheads and stone loach

Natural baits from the river, such as the fry of young dace, roach, minnows, and even little chub, all easily obtained with the landing-net from the shallows, make great chub baits.

Although these bottom-dwellers are seldom taken on rod and line, they form an important part of the chub's diet in most rivers, brooks and streams. Even ditches little more than a couple of feet wide and mere inches deep will breed both in profusion, and they will be hiding beneath every large flint, housebrick or item of junk which litters the bottom in clear-flowing water.

Simply place a net upright and hard against the bottom immediately behind any likely-looking hideout, and then gently lift the flint or brick upwards and to one side so

everything beneath is washed downstream by the current straight into the net. For a holding can, you can use a 1-gallon bait bucket, which can be hung on the belt thus keeping both hands free. When enough bait has been gathered, and only ever take enough for your own needs, they may be kept for a few days in a water butt or an aquarium with an aerator.

Bullheads and loaches can be trotted beneath a float in weir pools, ledgered on the bottom in deep, fast runs, or used as deadbaits and 'twitched' beside rafts and overhangs using freeline tactics. A size 4 hook through the top lip or nostrils secures them well for casting and banging into the chub.

Crayfish

While collecting bullheads and stone loach in streams still running fast, clear and pure over a clean gravel bottom, you will also catch the occasional crayfish, the largest of our freshwater crustaceans, which in every feature looks like a lobster. Once, most rivers in the British Isles

After sucking in two maggots on a size 16, this greedy 1 lb chub was found with a lamprey already in its throat. Tiny lampreys (ammocoete larva) are one of the finest natural baits readily available to the chub fisherman.

contained crayfish, and up until around the 1970/80s I would have urged you to try them for chub. As a summer bait, freelined into clear running water, their pulling power has no equal; but not now.

Unfortunately the saying 'when the crayfish disappear, the river won't be long afterwards', has come true all too often for minor rivers and streams in the past 20 years. Bore-hole water abstraction by farming and industry, greater quantities of treated and even untreated sewage, farming chemical run-off, each has taken its toll. Combined they have reduced clear flowing streams to ditches of effluent in which the crayfish is always the first to suffer. It is the barometer of pure water, and if a water you are fishing still contains numbers of crayfish, leave them be. Study the following pages covering the great diversity of chub baits that are available, happy in the knowledge that you are indeed privileged in having actually seen a live crayfish.

Lampreys

There are three separate species of this weird fish found in British freshwaters, the largest and most parasitic being the sea lamprey, which grows to over 3 ft long and enters freshwater in the late spring to lay its eggs in gravel beds similar to the salmon. I accidentally hooked one of these monsters while chub fishing the Dorset Stour at Throop Mill some while back, and made the mistake of putting it in the keep-net containing a chub and a tench. Within minutes the lamprey had clamped its powerful, plunger-type sucking mouth, full of sharp rasps, on to the side of the tench. A sharp bang on its head made it release its grip. The river lamprey, or lampern as it is sometimes called, is also migratory, and is a smaller version of the former, growing to around 15 in.

Brook lampreys are seldom longer than 6 in and never leave freshwater. They are generally found (whilst turning over the bottom looking for other natural baits) clinging to the underside of large stones or boulders, but while in their infant stage they live semi-dormant in soft silt or mud in a blind, toothless state. All three lampreys develop from the egg into blind, toothless 'ammocoete larva' 3 to 4 in long, and to say which is the larva of which lamprey is almost impossible.

To the chub fisherman, of course, it matters not because all three make fabulous baits and are most likely to be found in numbers amongst deep silt and mud banks such as are found immediately behind bridge supports or beneath tree roots. I have often found them in old pots or tin cans, or tyres lying on the bottom of the river, and they wriggle out when the silt is tipped out. In colour they are not dissimilar to a small eel, perhaps with a touch more beige or buff yellow.

Lampreys can be trotted beneath a float or freelined with the addition of a single AA or swan shot, and are just as effective when being retrieved. Present them on a size 6 or 4 tied direct, hooked once only through the mouth.

Baby eels

Better known as elvers, and at 3 to 4 in long only slightly thinner than a young lamprey, young eels are also fabulous natural baits for chub. Elvers are best collected with a fine-meshed net at night from mill and weir pools, where they collect around the sluices on their upstream migration by the thousands throughout the summer and early autumn. Pick the right night and one scoop is all you will need. Gently hook once only through the head or through the middle with a size 6 or 4 hook tied direct, and freeline or present beneath a heavy trotting float. Though a bait few anglers bother to use, elvers provide one of the most prolific natural sources of food to chub throughout the summer and autumn.

Minnows

Whether you obtain them from the gravel shallows with a minnow trap, or simply scoop out a bunch by swatting the water with a large, small-meshed landing-net, minnows are great baits for chub. They are an ideal size for chub to swallow, without prickly fins, and any chub from 10 in upwards will gulp them in and crush them with those powerful pharyngeal teeth before swallowing. Hook once only through the top lip or through both nostrils with a size 6 or 4 tied direct, and freeline your minnow or trot it down clear runs between beds of streamer weed. It is equally effective when ledgered static on the bottom of deep runs or weir pools, or cast beneath overhangs and retrieved erratically.

Caddis grubs

I can probably count on two hands the number of times since my childhood when I have needed to gather a supply of caddis grubs while stream fishing. Maggots, being easily available, make us all lazy. However, this free source of bait, slightly larger than a maggot, is always there, crawling slowly along the bottom in its protective case constructed from twigs, stones and sand particles.

There are, in fact, close on 200 different species of caddis, or to use its correct name – the sedge fly. You will find caddis grubs on fallen branches lying in the margins, or beneath large stones. To remove the grub, pinch the tail end gently to make the head and legs appear, then ease it out with your finger and thumb. One on a size 14 or three up on a size 10, trotted downstream between the weedy runs, or ledgered beneath weed-rafts, will quickly account for chub.

Having driven 20 miles to the river and forgotten the maggots, what do you do? You turn over large stones on the bottom or cast your eyes over submerged branches for the caddis grub. Remove it by pinching its tail and easing it out gently. It is one of the finest free, natural baits that nature provides.

BANKSIDE NATURALS

Slugs

If I were to pick one natural bait from all those readily available and most effective throughout the summer and autumn months, it would be the slug.

Being weighty, slugs can be freelined long distances without additional shots, although they work just as effectively when ledgered on the bottom of a deep, fast

Apart from being one of the most productive natural baits, an additional benefit with slugs is that they can be used to catch more than one chub.

pool or runs. Slugs can also be skate cast (in a series of skips just like skating flat stones into the sea) into awkward, mysterious spots beneath the low, overhanging branches of trees, where no other bait could be placed. Or they can be plopped in alongside long rafts of marginal rushes or sedges and retrieved in a twitching, popping mode just like a surface plug. They are the warm-weather chubbing bait par excellence. You nick a size 6 or 4 eyed hook tied direct to 6 lb test into one end of the slug – no more than is required for casting – leaving the entire point and barb exposed, otherwise the strike could be impaired and the hook not driven home.

Another benefit of fishing slugs is that being tough and durable, it is usually possible to catch more than one chub on the same bait before replacing it.

Contrary to popular belief, it is not difficult to keep slugs prior to using them. All you need is an old aquarium filled with fresh vegetation on to which fits a weighted sheet of gauze. Kept in a cool, darkened spot (on the garage floor) and topped up with fresh inmates every now and then, you will always have a supply at the ready. The main problem nowadays, with farming pesticides being so effective, is in collecting slugs in the first place. Many hedgerows where once you would have been guaranteed to obtain a tinful following heavy rain, especially after dark, now harbour very few. However, the undersides of larger stones in garden rockeries, damp cellars, the bottom of piles of old cut logs, in fact any rotten, damp hideout, will provide the habitat that slugs require. Damp woodlands well away from farming chemicals, such as public parks and overgrown pathways, are the places to visit. The best times are at night after heavy rain, or during the early morning when dawn is accompanied by thick fog or mist. At such times I have collected enough slugs for the morning's fishing from the pathway beside the river.

Of the 20 different species of British slugs, only three are useful for chub fishing as they grow in excess of 2 in, and are thus heavy enough for casting. They are the common red slug, easily identified by an orange frill on the underside of its brown body; the black slug, openly adored by chub fanatics; and the great grey slug, a beautiful creature flecked with dark brown markings over a pale grey body.

Snails

The slug is really only a snail without a shell, and I have on occasion, when slugs have been impossible to find, used large garden snails to good effect. You crush the shell gently, pulling off most of the broken pieces, and hook the somewhat squashed snail as though a slug. It cannot be cast very far, but will be swallowed by the chub with equal relish. I am sure (though I have yet to experiment along these lines) that chunks of freshwater swan mussel, or the meaty flesh of cockles available from the fish market, could be substituted for slugs. Anything and everything edible should be considered a potential chub bait.

Lobworms

Winter and summer, lobworms (large earthworms) will readily catch chub, whether freelined, twitched, trotted or ledgered. What is more, being a natural bait that chub see regularly, either because it crawls into the river, or because it enters the river by the thousands during flooding, the humble worm always has the edge over manufactured, well-used baits like bread and casters.

To collect a good supply of worms for storing, so they are always available during periods of drought, visit your local cricket pitch an hour after dark following several days of rain. In the winter, pick a mild evening, use a torch whose beam is not over bright and learn to walk slowly and tread softly. Hang a small bucket or bag around your neck so both hands are free, and refrain from awkward battles with worms refusing to leave their holes. Many of these 'stretched' worms die within a few days and could ruin a whole batch. If the ground is wet enough and the evening mild, there will be more than enough lying on the ground completely free of their holes.

Worm collecting is an evening out in itself, and not unexciting. Sometimes you come face to face with a family of hedgehogs or a policeman who believes you are up to no good. And on no less than two separate occasions, while concentrating only upon gathering enough worms, I have accidentally tripped over courting couples.

In the dim light of dawn, only his head and shoulders protruding above a thick marginal fringe of sweet reed grass, a chub enthusiast free-lines worms beneath overhanging willow along the opposite bank of the Upper Wensum near Norwich.

Large worms can be hooked once only through the head section with a size 6 or 4 tied direct to the reel line, or through the middle, which gives them added attraction when being retrieved in a series of twitches. For drifting a worm downstream to chub lying in shallow water beneath overhanging trees, try injecting a little air into the head of the worm. This technique stops it fouling on bottom weeds and produces fabulous, visible takes off the surface (fig. 10).

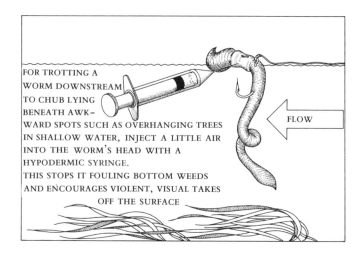

FOR TROTTING A WORM DOWNSTREAM TO CHUB LYING BENEATH AWK- WARD SPOTS SUCH AS OVERHANGING TREES IN SHALLOW WATER, INJECT A LITTLE AIR INTO THE WORM'S HEAD WITH A HYPODERMIC SYRINGE. THIS STOPS IT FOULING BOTTOM WEEDS AND ENCOURAGES VIOLENT, VISUAL TAKES OFF THE SURFACE

FLOW

FIGURE 10 *The floating worm*

Brandlings

Because these small, lively worms lack the weight required for freelining (a bunch plus a swan shot fixed 12 in up the line will do for close-range fishing), they are perhaps best considered for winter fishing and for long trotting once the weeds have gone. Tipped with a maggot or two, brandlings also make a fine cocktail bait for stret pegging or light ledgering in swims close into the bank. Three good-sized brandlings on a size 10 is about right. They are easily obtained from tackle shops pre-packed in containers, or from manure heaps that farmers pile by the roadside. Have the decency to ask whether you can gather a boxful first, and few farmers will refuse.

Wasp nests

There is a certain something about the sweet and sickly smell that emanates from the grub-laden cakes of a wasp nest which drives chub wild. You can use the large, fat,

To use it as both loose feed and hook bait, you need a good supply of wasp cake. A piece the size of a 50p coin, if heavy in grubs, is sufficiently heavy to be comfortably freelined.

white grubs singly or two up for trotting, and the mashed-up cake and grubs for groundbait, which works at any time in the season, even winter. The cakes (exactly the size of a round 2-pt bait tin) can be frozen until required. Or, and this is really a summer to autumn technique, large (50p-sized) pieces of cake heavy in grubs easily provide sufficient weight for freelining, just like presenting floating crust. A single grub fits nicely on to a size 14 hook and a piece of cake on to a size 6. The best way of obtaining freshly killed nests is to pay the local fruit farmer a visit from around July onwards, when he will be busy destroying the nests heavy in grubs. Most local councils also run pest control units from which nests may be obtained. Or when you discover a wasps nest in the river bank, or in the garden rockery, you can even have a go at removing it yourself, but do be very careful. The local chemist will supply special preparations for 'killing' the nest with explicit directions. These should be followed exactly.

Elderberries

The elder tree is particularly kind to the chub and to chub fishermen. It provides overhead shade all summer to the chub living beneath it, and in the autumn it provides succulent, purple-black berries for the chub to feed on, and from which the fisherman is able to brew a strong, fruity wine.

Harvest the berries before they become too soft, but not by stripping them. Remove lots of mini bunches, holding say 20 to 30 berries, with a pair of scissors, pack them gently into a pickling jar (any screw-top jar will suffice) without cramming them in. For preserving solution use either diluted formalin or glycerine. And while I have for years caught chub on berries used straight from the preserving fluid, it takes but a few minutes to rinse the bunches thoroughly before use.

Chub living permanently beneath large elder bushes will be ready to accept the berries at any time of the season. In other swims they may require encouragement from loose feed before switching on to the berries. To complement elderberries on the hook (and one fits perfectly on to a size

14), loose feed with stewed hempseed into which a handful or two of berries have been mixed.

OTHER NATURALS

Maggots

It must surely go without saying that maggots are a fine chub bait, and in all probability more chub are caught on them than any other bait. In many situations, however, because any fish from a minnow upwards can suck in even a bunch of maggots, they are on size alone not selective. During the warmer months, therefore, the maggot is a good bait choice only on rivers where the chub predominates and where large shoals of unwanted species are not present.

In the winter circumstances change drastically and the maggot really comes into its own, whether ledgered in conjunction with a block-end feeder or loose fed by hand when trotting. Small fish cease to be a problem in all but the mildest weather, and when temperatures approach zero with the river running clear, maggots are among the first choice because, being small, they will not overfeed the fish. Bronze or red maggots would appear to have the edge in extremely clear water over plain white, particularly in rivers that are heavily match-fished.

Casters

On certain rivers, particularly those running through the Midlands such as the Severn and Trent, casters are favoured over maggots by many chub fishermen. The juices and shells of a pint of casters crunched up and mixed into breadcrumb or cereal feed adds a certain something, whether distributed in a feeder or through balls of groundbait.

The 'tin lid' type of bait dropper is also useful for carpeting the bottom regularly with casters. It is especially effective in deep, fast, coloured rivers where chub are caught by trotting or stret pegging close in to the bank.

When using a single caster always endeavour to bury the small hook completely in it, rather than having the point protruding through the shell of the caster. It will look and behave as naturally as the loose feed around it, and will stand less chance of shattering until the chub sucks it back to its pharyngeal teeth.

As chub love the shade beneath overhanging elder trees, small wonder they acquire a liking for the juicy, purple-black berries. This fine bait is best trotted in conjunction with loose-fed, stewed hempseed.

Gently eased from the lawn on a damp evening and packed in moss, lobworms are effective when long trotted, static ledgered, or freelined naturally through the swim, especially when jerked or twitched on the retrieve.

Prawns and shrimps

Saltwater crustaceans prior to boiling and peeling are, both in colour and looks, a reasonable substitute for the crayfish. Large prawns have sufficient weight to be freelined (hook gently through the tail segment) and are also effective when trotted through weedy runs or ledgered.

Once boiled they turn bright pink and open up another avenue, whether peeled or unpeeled. The drawback is that when bites are slow in coming, you are quite liable to wade through a bag of peeled prawns in next to no time, just like luncheon meat cubes, so beware.

As the chub feasts on the albeit much smaller freshwater shrimp all year through, the flesh of peeled prawns and shrimps will be appreciated at any time. Loose-fed offerings regularly fed into the swim will induce the occupants into foraging for more. Peeled prawns and shrimps require careful casting and remain intact longer on smaller rather than larger hooks.

PARTICLE BAITS

Sweetcorn

During the summer months especially, sweetcorn can justifiably be included among the most magical of chub baits. Like other cyprinids, the chub is quickly stimulated into feeding by its stark yellow colour, texture and juices. Because it stays on so well, corn may be trotted, ledgered or stret pegged. With several kernels crammed on to a large hook, plus the addition of a swan shot 12 in up the line, it can even be freelined. I am not sure why, but its effectiveness is greater in clear water than coloured rivers. Sweetcorn sinks to the bottom quickly, and does not get washed out of the swim or pecked to bits by nuisance species, so loose feeding could not be easier.

In some rivers it has equal pulling power during the winter months, even when temperatures are at an all time low. In others you cannot buy a bite on sweetcorn until the following summer.

Stewed wheat

Use this excellent, inexpensive particle in exactly the same way as sweetcorn: one grain on a size 14 or three up on a size 10. To prepare (and this applies also to hemp and tares), put a few pints into a plastic bucket with a rip-off lid, cover by at least several inches with boiling water (to allow for massive expansion of the dry, hard grains) and push the lid on firmly.

After 24 hours excess water should be strained off, and the nutty-smelling kernels separated into polybags either for the freezer or for immediate use. As a change bait, should the chub become suspicious of plain wheat, just like sweetcorn it can easily be dyed bright red or orange. Simply add a spoonful of powder dye into the boiling water during preparation.

Hempseed

Though chub will accept stewed hempseed on the hook, it is most effectively used as an attractor and works wonderfully well when the river matures into winter. Loose feed little and often, and vary hook baits between maggots, casters, elderberry, tares and maple peas until one in particular outshines the rest. A single, darkish caster fished over hemp is deadly for chub in freezing cold, clear water conditions.

Tares

Prepare and present exactly as for stewed wheat and hempseed. This is a fine alternative bait best fished on light trotting tackle to shy, well-educated chub in rivers regularly match-fished. It can be used as both hook bait and loose feed, or just loose feed.

Nuts, beans and boilies

Baits originating from carp fishing, such as boilies, black-eyed beans and peanuts, are not usually instantly effective chub baits. However, they all find their way to the bottom of the river mixed in with attractor loose feeds such as hemp seed intended for pulling barbel into the swim, and chub are invariably first on the scene to sample the new food source. As additional quantities of a particular bait are introduced its pulling power over chub is increased, whether the barbel become hooked on it or not. The greedy chub capitalize on the situation every time. The implications of this are obvious. Just as peanuts, beans and boilies become deadly baits for chub once they have been pre-baited on a regular basis, any other carp bait should produce similar results.

As for carp, initially these hard baits are best side hooked, with the hook point and barb left completely free to penetrate. Should the chub in a particular swim wise up quicker than expected, there is no reason why the bait cannot be more sensitively presented, in which case the hair rig is the obvious answer.

PASTES

My favourite is cheese paste. It is especially effective in cold water during the winter, whether it is running clear or coloured. For this, soak half an old (two or three days old) loaf and after squeezing firmly to remove excess water, add an equal quantity of finely grated cheddar cheese and a sprinkling of parmesan, and knead into a firm, pliable paste.

Follow the same procedure to make a meaty paste. Swap the grated cheese for fresh sausagemeat, adding a teaspoon of marmite, bovril or crushed stock cubes for extra appeal.

Another smelly paste can be concocted from trout pellets or any pelleted pond-fish food. Simply reduce the pellets to a fine dust in a coffee-grinder and add water, kneading into a smooth, pliable paste. Plain bread paste will also catch chub, and is particularly effective when ledgered in conjunction with loose-fed mashed bread.

Whether stiffened with flour and kneaded into a firm paste, or mixed equal parts with bread paste, sausage-meat is much loved by chub. Large pieces can be freelined or ledgered.

BREAD FLAKE AND CRUST

When all else fails or when time prevents the preparation, purchase or gathering of alternative baits, you can always raid the breadbin. Fresh bread flake is as effective for ledgering in both clear and coloured fast rivers during the winter, as it is when freelined beneath rafts and down weedy runs during the brightness of a summer's day. In fact if I were limited to the use of a single chub bait covering both winter and summer fishing I would not hesitate to choose bread flake.

Bread crust is also an all-season winner. Floating crusts down stream is an exciting way of taking chub from the surface in both running and still waters, whilst a small cube of crust anchored to the bottom in freezing conditions will always produce at least a few knocks. Both forms also score well when searching for chub by long trotting, as the stark whiteness of bread is very visible.

Mashed bread

For attracting winter chub into a particular area or for switching resident fish into a feeding mood there is nothing to match the effectiveness of mashed bread.

*Don't waste tinned
cocktail sausages on
dinner guests, cut into
½ in segments and
give the chub a treat.*

Simply soak a whole batch of old bread scraps in a bucket
of water and squeeze out the excess. Ensure it is all well
and truly mashed between your fingers into thousands of
tiny particles. At this stage it may even be packed into
polybags and popped into the freezer for future use. A bag
is then removed on the evening prior to a morning's chub
fishing and left in the sink to thaw out overnight.

The reason for the success of well-mashed bread is that
even when it is introduced all day long it never overfeeds
the fish. This is because it separates into thousands of
small, fluffy pieces which, if not eaten, soon pass downstream and disintegrate. There is no other attractor
possessing even similar qualities.

MEATS AND CHEESES

Luncheon meat

The best way of presenting this fabulous bait (always keep
a tin or two in the tackle bag) is to cut it into suitable cubes
with a thin, long-bladed knife. Make sure the cubes are the
same length as the hook, then push the hook down
through the middle of the cube and pull it through at the
other end. Push the bend of the hook around the edge of

the cube, and gently pull on the line until the hook almost disappears back into the cube, and you have a bait that will cast well but which the hook will easily slice through on the strike. Because their fat content makes them fairly buoyant (some brands have a higher fat content and are more buoyant than others) always loose-feed cubes of meat a good way upstream so they settle on the bottom of fast swims exactly where you want them. To ensure that at least a few cubes end up near the bait, thread some on to a short PVA stringer which soon dissolves once the ledger has settled (fig. 11A). Luncheon meat cubes and the cubes from countless other solid meats (German, garlic-based sausage is an excellent one to try) can also be threaded on to a hair if bites presented directly on the hook prove impossible to hit.

Cubes of cheese

The harder or rubbery types of cheese like cheddar, edam and gouda work particularly well if presented on a ¾ in hair. Cut into ½ in cubes or use in mini-cube form, two or three up. Alternatively, use a cheese oblong and present it lengthways on the hair (fig. 11B). For loose-feed attraction cube a whole batch, and as with luncheon meat gauge how far upstream they need to be introduced in order to end up on the bottom of the swim close to the hook bait.

Tinned and cooked sausages

Frankfurters straight from the tin, or cooked sausages (pork, beef or spicy) are fabulous chub baits. They can be cut into cubes or oblongs and presented on a size 6 or 4 hook tied direct. Leave the skin on and sausage stays on the hook well in the fastest currents. As with other meats, sausage sections work well on a short hair whenever bites prove difficult to hit or are slow in coming. Loose feeding with sausage cubes could not be easier.

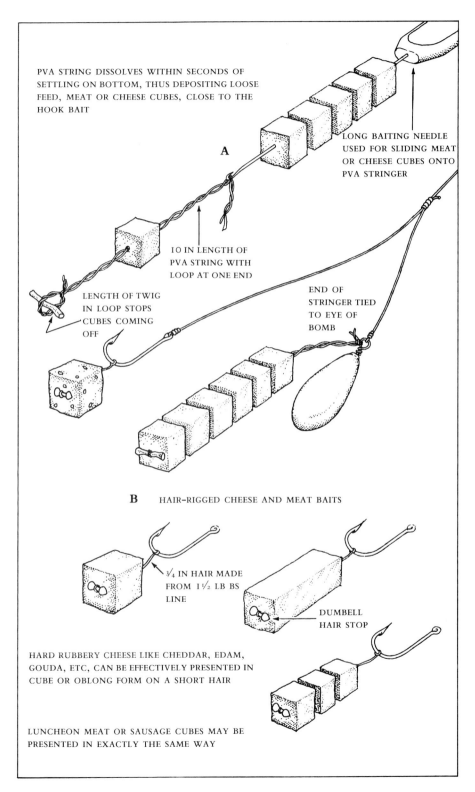

PVA STRING DISSOLVES WITHIN SECONDS OF SETTLING ON BOTTOM, THUS DEPOSITING LOOSE FEED, MEAT OR CHEESE CUBES, CLOSE TO THE HOOK BAIT

A

LONG BAITING NEEDLE USED FOR SLIDING MEAT OR CHEESE CUBES ONTO PVA STRINGER

10 IN LENGTH OF PVA STRING WITH LOOP AT ONE END

LENGTH OF TWIG IN LOOP STOPS CUBES COMING OFF

END OF STRINGER TIED TO EYE OF BOMB

B HAIR-RIGGED CHEESE AND MEAT BAITS

¾ IN HAIR MADE FROM 1½ LB BS LINE

DUMBELL HAIR STOP

HARD RUBBERY CHEESE LIKE CHEDDAR, EDAM, GOUDA, ETC, CAN BE EFFECTIVELY PRESENTED IN CUBE OR OBLONG FORM ON A SHORT HAIR

LUNCHEON MEAT OR SAUSAGE CUBES MAY BE PRESENTED IN EXACTLY THE SAME WAY

CHAPTER SIX

TECHNIQUES AND RIGS

FREELINING

Creeping up on an unsuspecting group of chub in clear water during the summer and autumn, and catching one on a completely freelined bait without any casting weight on the line other than that of the bait itself, is the most simple and arguably the most deadly method of all. However, it requires considerable stealth, and you may need to crawl the last few yards on all fours so as not to show your form against the sky line and scare the chub. Waders (those with supple uppers are particularly recommended) or a pair of rugged waterproof trousers are as much a part of the freeliners kit as the bait itself. Freelining also requires accurate casting, often into awkward, overgrown places because those are where the crafty chub loves to lie. For the wandering approach, using heavy baits and pulling out chub from overgrown jungle habitats, there is nothing to beat the standard top Avon rod with its all-through action (see 'Tackle', p. 45).

In trying to achieve maximum distance (to reach chub occupying a run on the opposite bank of a reasonably wide river) I occasionally punch the bait out with a double-handed cast. However, accuracy is more easily achieved by hooking the line over the ball of the forefinger to 'feel' the bait's weight) and casting with an underhand swing and flip. Provided that the spool is filled to the very lip, even with 5–6 lb test, the bait will fly effortlessly and accurately through the air until you 'feather' it down to land over the desired spot with the same finger. It is an art worth practising.

If you find this one-handed technique awkward or unsuitable, use the same underhand swing and flip, but hold a loop of line in your left hand (assuming the rod is in your right) and do a couple of pendulum swings with the

Charlie Clay knows all about the art of concealment, as he demonstrates while freelining bread flake through a streamy run close in to the bank of the beautiful Upper Wensum.

rod tip pointing at the target to build up momentum before letting go. The key is confidence, and using a bait which is heavy enough – a large slug, lobworm, cube of meat, a large piece of bread flake or cheese paste, and so on. All are perfect for freelining.

Because the bait appears to be untethered and behaves so naturally when either freefalling down to the bottom or being trundled along by the current, freelining outshines all other clear-water methods. The chub are not concerned by the diameter of a 6 lb line or its colour, or even by a large, visible hook. They are worried by unnatural movements and a suspicious-looking meal. Endeavour to leave a definite 'bow' in the line after closing the bale arm, allowing the bait to be carried downstream naturally by the current: through gravel runs between thick beds of flowing weed; into the darkness beneath floating rafts of cut weed or debris collected around the trailing branches of overhanging trees; down into the swirling cross-currents and eddies where a side stream enters the main stream; into the gloom beneath the low, overhanging brickwork of a road or rail bridge. There is almost no type of chub-attracting habitat that in warm, clear-water conditions cannot be effectively freelined.

When a chub grabs the bait and immediately belts off downstream to evade being pestered by others in the shoal, the line lifts across the surface and zings tight in the most unmistakable fashion, as though connected to a runaway lorry.

In swims with limited space, on the other hand, such as gaps between beds of bullrush or beneath tiny weed rafts, where the chub sucks the bait in and merely moves a few inches across current to maintain its position, visible line movement and therefore bite indication could be minimal – perhaps an initial 'twitch' (as the bait is engulfed) followed by a slow tightening, which in certain situations might well be mistaken for current pressure. You soon learn to know the difference so never take your eyes off the line as it is the best indicator of all.

A common occurrence when freelining the bait directly upstream is for the line momentarily to fall slack. This is caused by the chub moving a few feet downstream, but then returning to its original position. This is just as 'positive' an indication as the rod tip going over, so strike immediately and strike hard, quickly levering the chub away from the sunken tree or bullrush bed behind which it is hiding and into which it will surely try to bury the hook. Chub are masters of not only ridding themselves of the hook, but also transferring it into the closest snag. Keep the rod well up and in a full curve from the moment the hook goes home.

Should the line quite suddenly fall completely slack, this is because a chub is actually swimming downstream towards you with the bait. Quickly crank the reel a few times to pick up the loose line before slamming the hook home. These bites often occur instantly, within seconds of the bait hitting the surface, so you need to be watching that line like a hawk even before you close the bale arm. The most instant bites of all come to natural baits such as a large slug skipped or skate-cast across weed-beds covering the surface beneath low, overhanging branches where chub lie basking in an entanglement of subdued light. They are used to food like moths and caterpillars dropping from above, so virtually any item resembling an easy meal is instantly snapped up by the closest fish. Chub lying in seemingly impenetrable snags are nearly always attainable, but until you try you will never have the satisfaction of finding this out for yourself.

Although freelining for chub is most effectively accomplished by careful stalking along overgrown banks and manoeuvering yourself into a position from where a short cast can be made to fish lying between or beneath vegetation features, there are certain situations where wading is necessary. In diminutive, shallow, overgrown streams and rivers, you could easily frighten the chub long before a cast is made by taking to the water. In larger, overgrown and weedy, reasonably shallow rivers, where thick floating beds of potomogeton or water crowfoot clog the surface during midsummer, or impenetrable bankside trees separate you from chub which are visible, wading permits several casts to be made to chub that are completely unapproachable from the bank. Consider the situation, for instance, in fig. 12.

FIGURE 12 *By care-fully wading into centre of gravel shallows between weed-beds, you can offer a freelined bait to chub completely un-approachable from bank A*

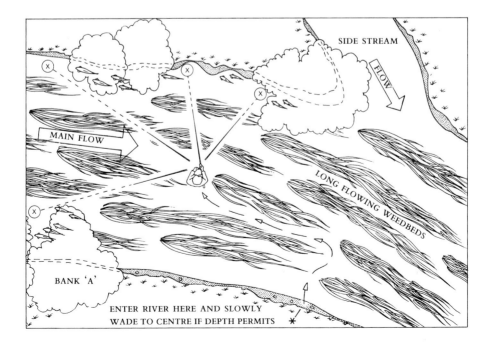

This shallow, weedy part of the river can only be effectively fished with a freelined bait. Here John flicks a large lump of bread flake to chub hugging the far bank beneath a tiny weed-raft.

Hit and run

Freelining for summer chub is hit-and-run fishing at its best. The commotion caused by hooking and landing or even losing one chub prised from a small group occupying a choice lie is usually enough to put the others down for a fair while. Make one or two more casts by all means, but don't be tempted to stay and labour on. With miles of twisting river and countless chub lies ahead, it is sacrilege not to wander about and explore everything on offer. A favourite old chub haunt of mine is a lovely, overgrown, 4-mile course of the Upper Waveney in Suffolk where the river does a massive U-bend all the way around Bungay Common. It is full of character, and I have walked and searched for the chub there for over 30 years, since they were first introduced into the Waveney from the River Wissey in the 1950s. And it is a fishery that is forever changing: through winter floods that reposition the silt beds, overhanging trees that die and are moved by the drainage department, seedling alders that from next to nothing in just three or four seasons lap the clear water and

Chub stalking is a mixture of opportunism, watercraft and stealth as this experienced fisherman proves. Only his head protrudes above the sparse bankside cover of nettles.

Freelining is very much a technique for warm, clear rivers. It makes use of the weight of natural baits, such as worms and slugs, to obtain maximum casting distance and reach fish occupying runs a long way downstream.

provide shelter to chub which quickly move into the dark runs beneath.

I have never counted the number of potential chub swims there, but during a morning's wandering I invariably end up plopping a bait into most of them. Unlike winter fishing, it is not how long you spend in the swim that counts. Providing you have crept up quietly and read the situation correctly, and providing the chub at that point in time are where you envisaged they would be, you should experience slamming bites within seconds.

During the summer months when the chub's metabolism is at its highest, the entire episode from kneeling down well back and upstream of an overhanging bush to slipping the hook from a 3 lb chub may take less time than it has taken me to write this. This is why freelining is very much a technique of warm, clear rivers where there is rarely the opportunity of enjoying a long fight with time to reflect how well the chub is performing. It is strike and haul fishing, where you must endeavour to bustle the chub away from its lair and into the net or pay the consequences.

Freelining becomes less practical once the weeds have been killed off by the first severe frosts of winter and water temperatures have lowered the chub's metabolic rate, making it less inclined to move several feet for a bait.

Very occasionally the river may even run slow enough during the winter months for a freelined bait to reach bottom where the chub are lying, and in very mild conditions a bite could develop soon afterwards. But the chub will not show the speed or the same aggression of summer. A swan shot or two could be added to anchor the bait on the bottom, but then by not permitting the flow to work the bait naturally through the swim you are not strictly freelining.

Nevertheless, the addition of a large shot, say 12 inches from the bait, does allow you to keep in touch in these awkward situations when the flow is too strong or variable for straight freelining yet insufficient to warrant a ledger link. And where large baits like a lump of meat, cheese paste or lobworms are concerned, a single shot on the line does not inhibit the chub. With worms the shots can even help induce takes on the retrieve because it imparts an attractive, fluttering, downwards movement whenever you pause momentarily.

LEDGERING

Rod-top ledgering

A natural progression from freelining is to add weight to the bait, either for casting or for anchoring it down in a particular spot, or both, and watch the rod top for bite indication. Because of the water pressure of really fast runs, whether shallow or deep, in large powerful rivers such as the Severn or Wye, a 1 oz bomb or more may be required to nail the bait to the bottom. A similar situation exists in all rivers, even comparatively small ones such as the fast, swirling waters of weir pools where, unless the bait stays put until the chub locate it, the force of the current will simply wash it downstream to an unproductive area.

As with freelining, the ideal rod is the standard-top Avon, which should be held during the summer months when bites are liable to be quick in öming. Whether standing or sitting, hold the rod firmly with two fingers either side of the reel stem and your entire forearm supporting the handle. After casting, and once the ledger has settled in the desired spot, make a habit of hooking your forefinger (at the first joint) around the line. Once adopted, you will find this a particularly sensitive and comfortable way of keeping the rod still. There is nothing to stop you from using a front rod rest, which helps steady the tip, especially in windy conditions and extremely fast water. You will quickly come to recognize the line tightening across your forefinger as the rod tip knocks.

When you cast downstream, the rod tip will be pulled round by the chub if they in turn move downstream with the bait. If the chub simply moves across the current, however, the tip might suddenly relax or spring back immediately following a gentle knock (see p. 97).

When casting directly upstream to chub, use only enough weight to hold bottom so that when a fish sucks in the bait and turns around, the bomb is dislodged causing the line to fall slack immediately. These are great bites to hit, but remember that, as when freelining, you need to lift the rod back in a long, hard, sweeping strike to straighten the line and bang the hook home.

During the autumn, chub respond aggressively to small fish like minnows and gudgeon. Hook once only through the nostrils with a size 4 hook and trot beneath a float, or bump it downstream across the current on a ledger rig.

For loose-feeding chub in any appreciable flow, the block-end feeder allows a slow dispersal of baits such as maggots. A simple fixed paternoster rig works best.

It is best to use the minimum amount of lead needed to hold bottom for ledgering downstream. It allows you to inch the bait down and across the bottom by raising the rod tip every so often in order to search the swim thoroughly (fig. 13). This imparts a certain amount of life to the bait and often promotes an instant bite. There are times when chub will only accept a completely static bait and times when, unless it is constantly on the move like the unattached offerings thrown in to attract fish, they will show not the slightest interest. So always be willing to experiment and to work the bait along.

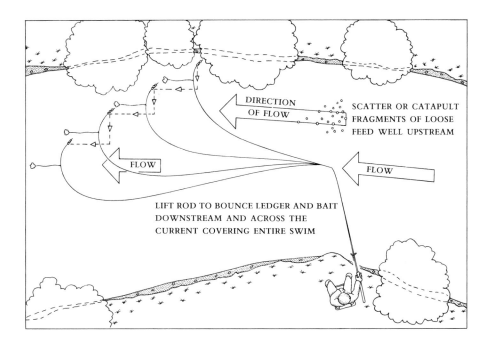

For heavy water ledgering a 5 or 6 lb line is ideal. Resist the temptation to make up complicated ledger rigs. Running ledgers with swivels, split rings and non–tangle tubing may look acceptable on paper, but in reality work no better than a simple fixed paternoster (fig. 14). I would in fact say that as all the various bits tend to collect weed, running ledgers are inferior to the fixed paternoster described.

Simply tie on a 10 in length of mono (reel line), using a four-turn water knot, 20 in above the hook. To this, fix either an Arlesey bomb or enough swan shots to just hold

FIGURE 13 *Rod-top ledgering. Work the bait downsream, using just enough weight to hold bottom when rod is held high.*

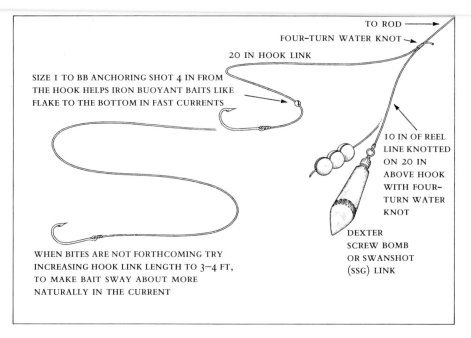

TO ROD ⟶

FOUR-TURN WATER KNOT

20 IN HOOK LINK

SIZE 1 TO BB ANCHORING SHOT 4 IN FROM
THE HOOK HELPS IRON BUOYANT BAITS LIKE
FLAKE TO THE BOTTOM IN FAST CURRENTS

10 IN OF REEL
LINE KNOTTED
ON 20 IN
ABOVE HOOK
WITH FOUR-
TURN WATER
KNOT

DEXTER
SCREW BOMB
OR SWANSHOT
(SSG) LINK

WHEN BITES ARE NOT FORTHCOMING TRY
INCREASING HOOK LINK LENGTH TO 3–4 FT,
TO MAKE BAIT SWAY ABOUT MORE
NATURALLY IN THE CURRENT

FIGURE 14 *Simple fixed paternoster*

bottom. Swan shots are more practical because it takes seconds to either add or subtact one for fine adjustment. For currents requiring in excess of five or six swan shots, bombs are advisable. The brass screw design are good because they make a quick change of weight easy. Attention to little things such as continually changing the ledger weight to suit the current force of each swim as you move up or down river, may seem unnecessary, but will be reflected by more fish in the net.

Buoyant bait like bread flake does not always settle on the bottom in really strong currents; it tends to flap about and look unnatural. Sometimes the chub gobble it up for this very reason, and at such times an increase in the hook length to 3 or even 4 ft will encourage more confident bites. On other occasions it is refused for the same reason. Experiment by adding an anchoring shot just 4 in from the bait, which will ensure it settles statically.

Worms and hard baits such as cheese are ideal fast-water offerings. They stay on a large hook well, and withstand the attentions of unwanted nuisance species. Also worth trying, particularly during the autumn, is a small fish such as minnow, bleak, gudgeon or stone loach. Hook once only through the top lip or through both nostrils, and fish as any other bait. If little interest is shown when the fish is presented hard on the bottom, bump it downstream every so often by lifting the rod tip to dislodge the lead and lowering it again. And be ready for a really slamming take as you do so. Chub grab small fish with considerably more force than they do paste baits. In weedy or particularly snaggy parts of the river don't bother to present the fish live. Tap it sharply on the head before casting and you won't have to worry about it hiding or swimming into snags. Alive or dead, it will be sucked in by the chub just the same. For additional bait ideas see the chapter on baits.

With freelining and rod-top ledgering techniques using largish baits, indications on the line or the rod tip are likely to be most positive during the summer and autumn months. As the season progresses and much colder weather sets in, a different approach is required. No longer will the chub instantly respond to large, moving offerings. In low water temperatures especially, smaller baits will be the order of the day, which leads to much smaller bite registrations. And to identify smaller indications the finely tapered tip of the Avon quiver-tip rod is the answer (see p. 45).

Quiver tip ledgering/Feeder fishing

In slow-moving, clear rivers that are regularly match-fished, chub learn from their mistakes and become very wary. This leads on occasion to their accepting only small baits like casters or maggots presented static on a tiny hook. After dark, however, the situation improves dramatically (see p. 101).

The mouth of even a 2 lb chub (which is a comparatively small specimen) looks ridiculous when compared to the size of an 18 hook. It is indeed difficult to believe that the same chub will without fear or favour gobble up a fat slug freelined on a size 4 hook direct to 6 lb test in August, yet four months later takes its time in cold water to approach and sip in a single maggot on a size 20 to a pound bottom.

Fortunately, chub do not become too choosey to be caught on ultra-fine tackle, even on heavily fished rivers. Look to see if the banks are well trodden wherever you fish, and consider tactics accordingly when standard methods and baits do not produce.

With the bait quivertip-ledgered close in to the near bank and his arm resting comfortably along the rod handle, this chub fisherman is perfectly poised to hit the tiniest of bites.

In large or deep rivers where the flow is considerable, where loose feed introduced either by hand or catapult stands little chance of coming to rest on the bottom close to the hook bait, a swimfeeder rig used in conjunction with the Avon quiver-tip rod is a deadly combination.

For wide, slow rivers, pack loose feed like sweetcorn, casters, small meat cubes or maggots into the middle of a metal-cage or plastic open-end feeder and seal with a dampened plug of breadcrumbs at each end. In any sort of appreciable flow the block-end feeder is invaluable because it allows a slow dispersal of baits like maggots and casters. When chub are not likely to move quickly on to the hook bait, during sub-zero winter conditions, for instance, you do not want all the loose feed to be instantly whisked away downstream. Resist the temptation to use complicated feeder rigs. The basic fixed paternoster is ideal for all chub ledgering, and is quickly constructed by joining the hook

Unlike many species, chub do acclimatize to really severe weather conditions and while bites may often be reduced to the tiniest of pulls, drop backs and twitches, bite they will. Knowledge of the exact whereabouts of each chub shoal (hence the benefit of summer exploration and location) is half the battle, because chub will not want to follow mashed bread or maggots from 50 yd down river in sub-zero weather.

Despite a liberal helping of snow, an unfriendly river and freezing fingers, happiness is undoubtedly chub-shaped. What else could be caught against such adversaries.

A deep love of cold water chubbing comes with age, and is a direct result of having done time fishing and caught a great many chub in younger days. That famous immortal saying of my old mate, Fred J. Taylor, 'I'll be glad when I've had enough of this' just about sums up arctic chubbing and could not be more explicit. Yet we still sit there.

Mention of Fred J. takes me back to the 1950s and early 1960s, when his exploits after chub on the then lovely reaches of the Upper Great Ouse at Stony Stratford and Beachampton with his brother Ken, cousin Joe and the late Dick Walker, were regularly related in the angling press. *The* method for winter chubbing in those days regardless of weather severity was to ledger small cubes of bread

crust and cheese with an Arlesey bomb stopped just 2 in
from the hook with a split shot. Invariably it produced
very hittable bites with the rod tip really banging round
(there were no built-in quiver tips in those days). Rods
were even on occasion known to fly from the rests and
crab along the bank for several yards because in many cases
the chub had in fact hooked itself. Twenty years ahead of
its time (although they did not realize it then) the Taylor
brothers were using the 'bolt rig' to deadly effect. These
tactics are always worth trying in low temperatures when
chub are loathe to move about much, but watch out for
those rod-tip wrenching bites once the chub feels the bomb
stopped only 2 in from the bait.

Floodwater quiver tipping

Fig. 7 (p. 40) shows how chub will tuck close into the
bank behind all their usual habitats and even move position
completely during flood conditions. They dislike having
to face a continual barrage of fast, dirty flood water,
particularly that caused by snow which has been lying
around for some time before draining into the river.

Quieter waters and the shelter provided by cattle drinks,
ditches or side streams, which under normal conditions
chub could not even navigate, will now play host to them.
Long slacks close into the bank situated immediately
below acute bends will also contain numbers of chub. In
each case, you should sit well back from the water's edge
to fish. Introduce into the head of the swim a little mashed
bread or broken worm fragments and follow in with
quiver-tipped flake, cheese paste, a lobworm or a bunch of
maggots. To catch flood-water chub you often need to
present the bait at ridiculously close range, so net each fish
with the minimum of disturbance and either retain them or
return them well away from the swim

Quiver tipping at night

Summer or winter, when trying to extract chub from very
hard-fished stretches or from very shallow or clear flowing
water, there is no doubt that fishing after dark greatly

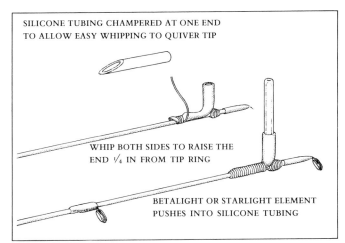

FIGURE 18 Quiver tipping at night

increases your chances. Bites become far more positive when the chub's natural caution and fear becomes suppressed as darkness looms over the river valley.

To ensure that bites on the quiver tip are visible in the dark you can whip a $\frac{3}{4}$ in section of silicone tubing on to the very tip and push in a luminous betalight element or a starlight (which is much brighter but only last 6–8 hours) (fig. 18).

The tip can also be illuminated with a narrow torch

FIGURE 19 Quiver tipping at night

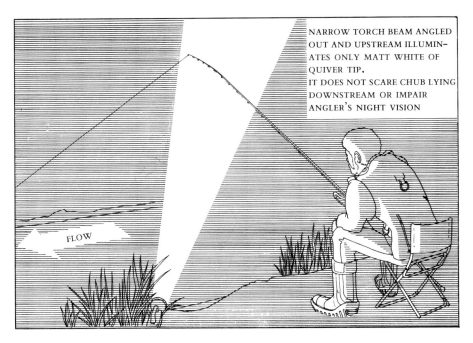

When flood waters rise above the banks and spew over the fields, chub can be caught close in to the bank immediately downstream of acute bends or below bridge supports – behind any obstruction which offers them shelter out of the main flow.

beam, which is one of the reasons why I paint the last 16 in of the quiver tip matt white. Watching the tip, even for several hours, in the dark then becomes most pleasurable, and there is no danger of eye strain. And provided that the torch is positioned downstream of the tip and angled to shine both out and upwards towards the rod (which should be supported on two telescopic rod rests), its beam will never scare away the fish or spoil your night vision (fig. 19). Also keep a tiny pocket torch handy for undoing tangles.

One final word about quiver-tip ledgering, which applies as much to daytime fishing as it does to fishing at night, and that is on striking. Rather, it is about the angle to the water at which the rod is positioned on the rests, because in terms of line pick up and setting the hook, this is of paramount importance (fig. 20). Only for really close-range ledgering, for instance, should the rod be positioned straight out in front of you, as in fig. 20A. It is much better to angle the rod downstream towards the fish as this results in greater line pick up on the strike, as illustrated in fig. 20B, provided that the angler sits facing in the direction of the rod.

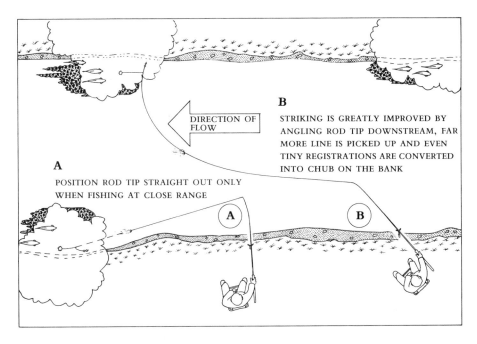

FIGURE 20 *Striking when ledgering*

FLOAT FISHING

Waggler trotting

Easing the bait downstream to chub in wide, slow, coloured rivers such as the Nene, Warwickshire Avon or Middle Great Ouse, is a lovely way of catching them at any time of the season. But it does necessitate the use of much lighter tackle than for ledgering or freelining. Along parts of the river that are regularly fished by clubs, where chub see the fisherman's bait every weekend, they learn to bite incredibly shyly and if the rig is insensitive, not at all.

I also like to use the waggler for delicately presenting small baits like maggots and casters to chub in the smaller rivers during the winter, when the weeds have gone provided that the flow is not too strong. In clear, low, cold water conditions when chub in shallow rivers tend to pack beneath definite habitat swims like overhanging or sunken willows (fig. 5, p. 33) and are loathe to leave such protection, there are times when, unless the bait is teased into spots no ledger could ever reach directly under the edge of the branches, you won't catch any chub.

With the float set to present the bait just off bottom it is

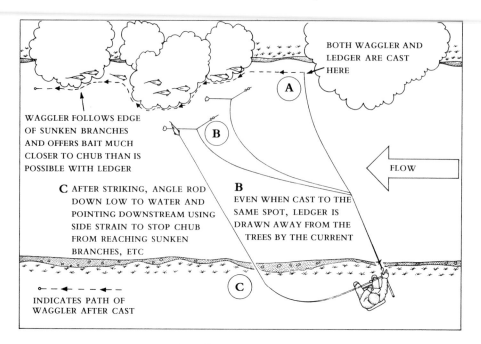

BOTH WAGGLER AND LEDGER ARE CAST HERE

A

B

WAGGLER FOLLOWS EDGE OF SUNKEN BRANCHES AND OFFERS BAIT MUCH CLOSER TO CHUB THAN IS POSSIBLE WITH LEDGER

FLOW

C AFTER STRIKING, ANGLE ROD DOWN LOW TO WATER AND POINTING DOWNSTREAM USING SIDE STRAIN TO STOP CHUB FROM REACHING SUNKEN BRANCHES, ETC

B EVEN WHEN CAST TO THE SAME SPOT, LEDGER IS DRAWN AWAY FROM THE TREES BY THE CURRENT

C

INDICATES PATH OF WAGGLER AFTER CAST

FIGURE 21 *Using waggler for presenting bait to winter chub beneath overhanging and sunken trees*

cast a few feet upstream from the trees (fig. 21A) and allowed to be carried downstream unchecked alongside the branches. Any attempt to keep a tight line, as with the ledger (fig. 21B), will draw the bait away from the fish. Remember the very second a fish is hooked to angle the rod over, low to the water and pointing downstream to apply maximum side strain to a chub that is bent on snagging your hook amongst sunken roots and branches.

With an easy-actioned waggler rod (see p. 44) coupled to a 2½ lb test line, even with size 16 or 18 hooks it is surprising just how much pressure can be applied in this way. And if the hook pulls out, regard it philosophically.

In wider, deeper, slower rivers where swims are more open and deeper channels often run down the centre of the river, terminal tackle can be reduced further. To induce bites in really cold water step down to a 1¼–1½ lb hook link and an 18 or 20 hook, or even a 22 hook. I do not like to play chub on ultra-fine tackle, but I do appreciate the need for using it in order to promote bites and at least stand the chance of landing shy chub on small baits – as opposed to sitting there biteless using heavy tackle.

Loose feed should be kept to a minimum initially and should be catapulted well upstream to allow for current speed. If baiting with a single caster or maggot, stewed hempseed or tares are excellent loose feed attractors, but feed sparingly in very cold conditions. Just half a dozen seeds every other trot down will suffice.

An elderberry on the hook (see p. 72) works especially well when loose feeding hemp, tares or casters, and generally produces a noticeably slower bite.

Whether fishing close in or far out, or in very slow or medium-paced water, the main difference in the waggler rig is purely one of shotting (fig. 22). You will notice from the diagram that only straight peacock wagglers are recommended because the large buoyant tip allows a single caster or maggot to be fished well over depth and slowly drawn along the bottom, whereas the fine tip of an insert waggler would be pulled under.

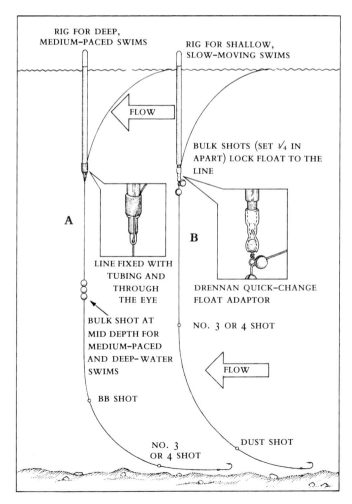

RIG FOR DEEP, MEDIUM-PACED SWIMS

RIG FOR SHALLOW, SLOW-MOVING SWIMS

FLOW

BULK SHOTS (SET ¾ IN APART) LOCK FLOAT TO THE LINE

A

B

LINE FIXED WITH TUBING AND THROUGH THE EYE

DRENNAN QUICK-CHANGE FLOAT ADAPTOR

BULK SHOT AT MID DEPTH FOR MEDIUM-PACED AND DEEP-WATER SWIMS

NO. 3 OR 4 SHOT

BB SHOT

FLOW

NO. 3 OR 4 SHOT

DUST SHOT

FIGURE 22 *Waggler trotting rigs*

John's arm stretches out to net a good chub caught waggler trotting on his local River Wensum.

The main difference between the two rigs shown is that fig. 22A is for trotting deep swims or those with a medium pace, with the bulk shot set at around mid depth, so the float is attached by a length of silicone tubing. That in fig. 22B is for fishing slow swims. The bulk shot locks the float to the line, leaving just two small shots down near the hook.

Long trotting

I love long trotting for chub, especially in the smaller rivers. It is such a good probing, searching, exploring method, and works best during mild winter weather when with the weed growth gone, chub keep permanently on the look out for food items brought down to them by the current. In really heavy water I use the standard-top 11–12 ft Avon rod coupled to a 4 lb test line, but for most other situations a 13 ft waggler rod does fine.

Line is 2½ to 3 lb with hooks in sizes 14 to 10 tied direct for a wide variety of baits from maggots to small cubes of bread crust.

Because it has such a wide tip and is easily seen even at distances of up to 30 yd, and because for its stumpy size it carries a good shotting load, for most long trotting I use a chubber. In fast water there is no point whatsoever in messing about with complicated shotting rigs, especially in water less than 4 ft deep. Simply put the entire shotting load within 1 ft of the hook, so the bait is presented right down where the chub are (fig. 23A). In swims of considerable depth where the pace is moderate, bunch the bulk shot within 3 ft of the hook and pinch on a BB or an AA in between (fig. 23B).

To some, long trotting is the ultimate technique. Bruce Vaughan searches for chub with the float around a long bend edged with reeds and sedges on a carrier of the lovely River Kennet.

I prefer to slightly overshot these chunky floats and keep a fairly tight line as they are taken downstream by the flow: alongside overhanging trees, around the back eddies in weir pools, through deep centre channels, around acute bends overhung by willows and so on. It is very much a moving game whereby carrying the minimum of tackle, I can offer the bait to chub inhabiting numerous interesting and demanding swims along the river's twisting course. I avoid all areas of heavy turbulence and extreme shallows, preferring the long, easy-paced glides where experience suggests that chub are most likely to be shoaled up.

FIGURE 23 *Long trotting*

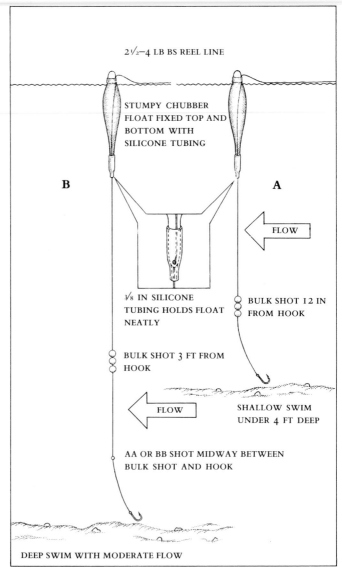

2½–4 LB BS REEL LINE

STUMPY CHUBBER FLOAT FIXED TOP AND BOTTOM WITH SILICONE TUBING

B

A

FLOW

⅜ IN SILICONE TUBING HOLDS FLOAT NEATLY

BULK SHOT 12 IN FROM HOOK

BULK SHOT 3 FT FROM HOOK

FLOW

SHALLOW SWIM UNDER 4 FT DEEP

AA OR BB SHOT MIDWAY BETWEEN BULK SHOT AND HOOK

DEEP SWIM WITH MODERATE FLOW

There is nothing to match mashed bread, with either flake or small cubes of crust for the hook, as loose feed for coloured water. In clear water, on the other hand, maggots or casters have the edge, though brandlings will on occasion score heavily. It is a matter of horses for courses and provides a wonderful roaming game with a bait pouch belted around the waist, plus extra shots, hooks and floats in my waistcoat. I like to think that impatience when long trotting can on the right day catch more chub than sitting in one spot.

Stret pegging

This deadly method of float ledgering in running water only works for chub occupying swims close into the bank alongside matted rafts of sweet reed grass or rushes, or beneath overhanging bushes and trees. Where the weed growth is not over thick, stret pegging is a good way of fishing over marginal gravel runs during the summer. However, it is during the winter when, through sheer force of flow, marginal swims become packed with chub that this technique really comes into its own.

The set up is ridiculously simple, but you must understand the principle by which it works (fig. 24). To start with, the float (owing to its buoyancy a medium-sized straight peacock waggler is perfect) must be fixed top and bottom and set considerably deeper than the swim. This is to allow for the belly that forms in the line between float and shots. And it is this pressure-absorbing belly or bow in the line that stops the float from cocking and being pulled under by the force of the current. If the flow does occasionally cock the float, it has been set too shallow so push it up about 1 ft or so. In gentle currents a single swan

FIGURE 24 *Stret pegging*

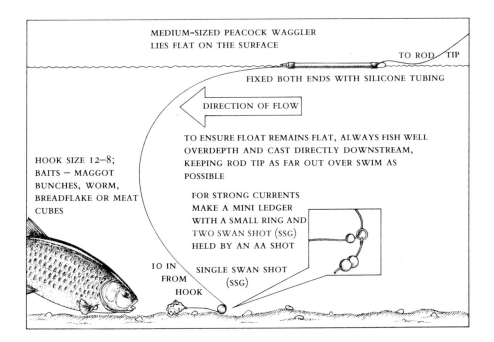

MEDIUM–SIZED PEACOCK WAGGLER LIES FLAT ON THE SURFACE

TO ROD TIP

FIXED BOTH ENDS WITH SILICONE TUBING

DIRECTION OF FLOW

TO ENSURE FLOAT REMAINS FLAT, ALWAYS FISH WELL OVERDEPTH AND CAST DIRECTLY DOWNSTREAM, KEEPING ROD TIP AS FAR OUT OVER SWIM AS POSSIBLE

HOOK SIZE 12–8; BAITS – MAGGOT BUNCHES, WORM, BREADFLAKE OR MEAT CUBES

FOR STRONG CURRENTS MAKE A MINI LEDGER WITH A SMALL RING AND TWO SWAN SHOT (SSG) HELD BY AN AA SHOT

10 IN FROM HOOK

SINGLE SWAN SHOT (SSG)

*Stret pegging close in
to the bank after dark
with soft cheese paste,
using a powerful beta-
light float rig, resulted
in this fine winter
chub for John.*

shot pinched on 10 in from the hook will suffice. For fast
swims make up a mini 2 swan shot ledger using a tiny ring
on 1 in of line, and stop it 10 in above the hook with an AA
shot. The secret of stret pegging is to ensure that the float
is set well enough over depth, and to cast directly
downstream with the rod tip as far out over the water as
possible. The float will then settle immediately downstream of the rod tip. Hold the rod pointing downstream
and across, or set on two rod rests almost horizontal,
perhaps with the tip angled slightly upwards.

Bites often start with a gentle shaking of the flat float (as
the chub inhales the bait) followed by a positive slide
under. This is because the resistance from the float's buoyancy is not felt straight away as with trotting, but only
when it is too late. So the bait is taken with relish even by
spooky chub. It is a delightful way of float fishing which,
once perfected, you will want to use close into the bank.

Using the stick float to present casters down a narrow run between thick weed-beds on Norfolk's River Wensum, well-known author and illustrator Dave Batten proves the method's effectiveness.

Stret pegging at night

To enjoy this method after dark when the chances of contacting specimens or difficult clear-water chub are greatly increased, simply glue in a luminous betalight element of 600 microlamberts into the top of the waggler and whip around the joint for strength. Or add a short length of silicone tubing to the float tip and push in a starlight luminous element, which is very much brighter although it only lasts 6–8 hours.

Stick-float fishing

In cold-water conditions when presenting maggots or casters on ultra-fine tackle to suspicious chub, and whenever there is a flat calm or a gentle upstream wind, a stick float slightly overshotted so the tip is a mere blimp in the surface and is gently held back, will induce bites when other ways of trotting do not. But there is a catch. You can really only present the stick float accurately at close range and certainly no further than the rig can be cast underarm – distances of up to about two rod lengths out and no more.

Presentation is of course best when the float is being trotted in deepish water immediately downstream of, and in a direct line with, the rod tip. By holding gently back on the overshotted float tip you will not pull the bait across the current but float it up from the bottom in a most enticing fashion, just like the loose feed around it.

Loose feed of stewed hempseed with a hook bait of single bronze maggot or caster is a deadly combination beneath a stick float.

FLOATER FISHING

Some would say the most exciting way of catching chub during the summer, when weed-beds furrow the surface and make other methods impractical, is with floating crust or wasp cake. There are two ways of enjoying floater fishing; either using a completely free line or with the addition of a controller float like the ten-pin. For close-range swims a completely free line treated with mucilin so it floats easily and does not hinder the bait's passage downstream is all that is required. A fairly large hook is best for crust, and a size 6 or 4 (depending on bait size) is ideal. There is more than sufficient weight in a 10p-sized piece of crust for casting and if you think not, simply dunk it momentarily.

Floating crust

To entice chub up to the surface, away from the cover of weed-beds or overhung hideaways, and to persuade them to suck in crusts confidently, sit or crouch well upstream of the swim and introduce a batch of loose crusts into midstream every couple of minutes. Half a dozen at a time will do nicely. Don't worry if the first few batches are ignored (you need at least a couple of large tin-loaves for a morning's crusting), it is all part of the ritual or game anglers and chub play with each other. Sooner or later up will come a huge pair of lips, and in a huge oily swirl down will go one of the crusts, then another and so on. Float your crusts down until each crust disappears when it reaches a certain spot. Then put your hook in the next crust. It is just like floater fishing for carp, probably the most heart-stopping technique of all.

When the first swim dries up because too many chub have been removed or you botched the first strike and put them all down, wander downstream following your batches of previously uninspected crusts, some of which by now will have attracted chub in other spots.

Wasp cake

As an alternative and wonderful change bait to floating crust, try fishing in the same way with wasp cake (see p. 71). It has magical qualities and will, if you have enough cakes to break up for loose feeding the chub into a frenzy, pave the way to some memorable hauls of summer chub.

It has a sweet, honey-like smell to which the chub quickly becomes addicted. Once aroused, chub will charge several feet through clear water to intercept a piece of floating cake ahead of other shoal members. It is therefore a most selective bait because as long as your cast puts a piece of cake alongside a noted specimen, unless you strike too early it is as good as in the net. As with bread crust, always wait for the fish's lips to fully close and for it to get its head down beneath the surface and the line to tighten before banging home the hook. As with freelining other baits a 5–6 lb line is mandatory.

Controller fishing

To drift the bait into distant swims without the current bellying the free line into an unstrikable situation, the answer is to thread on a small loaded controller (like the ten-pin) which adds weight for casting (smaller baits can

*Despite Wilson giving
it some 'wellie' with
the full force of an
Avon rod and 6 lb
test, a big chub makes
a dive for freedom
beneath a weedraft on
its way upstream,
having sucked in float-
ing crust over 30 yd
downstream.*

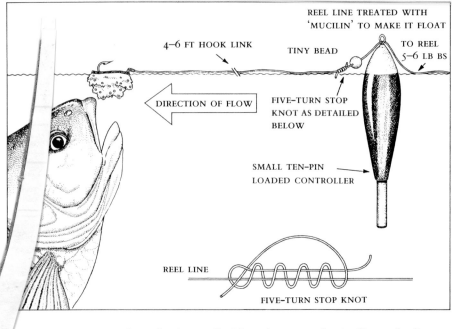

FIGURE 25 *Floating controller fishing*

then also be used). More importantly, it allows the line to be mended occasionally while the bait floats ahead downstream without it being pulled off course.

Stop the ten-pin 4 to 6 ft above the hook with a nylon stop knot and small bead (fig. 25).

Floater fishing in stillwaters

Except for small overgrown lakes and pits, in which freelined crusts can be placed or drifted alongside bushes or sunken trees close to the chub's hideouts, the loaded controller offers the most effective way of getting the bait out to chub patrolling the surface. Loose attractor crusts should be catapulted well upwind around the float and the entire batch allowed to drift naturally with the wind or surface pull.

Keep paying out line as though trotting. Every now and then lift any bowing line off the surface with the rod held high, and lay or flick it upwind so that it is reasonably straight again. When fishing really large waters you have to decide on a point beyond which striking would be impaired because of the possibility of pricking and losing a chub. So strike the crust off and retrieve for a new cast.

Livebaiting

For trotting tiny fish like minnows or the fry of any small shoal fish beneath a float, a 2 to 3 swan shot chubber fixed to a 5 to 6 lb line both top and bottom should suffice. Set it to present the bait 1 to 2 ft above the bottom with the bulk shot set 1 ft above the hook.

For larger fish, such as a 3 to 4 in bleak, gudgeon, bullhead, small dace or lamprey, use a ¾ in diameter pilot float plugged to the line with 1 in of fine peacock quill.

Use a size 6 hook for minnows and a 4 for larger baits, hooking them once only through the top lip or through both nostrils. Trot steadily downstream holding back every so often to waver the bait tantalizingly up and away from the bottom.

Summer live-baiting can produce hectic results, especially at the tail end of large weir pools and in the back eddies where chub gather in large shoals. Trot the bait beside all the usual habitats along the opposite bank, remembering to let it swing across the current at the very end of the run so it finishes up in the margins along your own bank. Then retrieve it gently in slow pulls plus the occasional twitch, ready for a take at any moment.

Generally speaking, if a chub is going to grab hold of the bait, that first run through the swim offers the most likely chance so move on after giving each spot two or three casts.

When the float does suddenly shoot under and the line tightens, you are on your own. If you strike immediately you will pull the hook from a percentage of fish, and if you leave the run to develop you could still pull it out or have the bait returned minus its lower half. In short, there is no set formula guaranteed to hook chub on live baits, which is why nowadays I strike as soon as the float goes in a long sweep of the rod. I keep it fully bent as the chub shakes its head, hoping the hook will find a purchase. If anything, winter live-baiting has the edge, and is particularly effective in very cold, clear-water conditions when jack frost has painted everything white and most other methods are less effective.

Sometimes small jack pike become a nuisance and every so often bite the hook off, which might just sway you into

Chub will attack most surface-popping and diving plugs, thus offering a whole new, exciting approach to weedy, overgrown parts of the river during the summer months.

using a wire trace, but resist the temptation. Far fewer
chub will suck in the live bait as a result, and pike rid
themselves of a large single hook unbelievably easily.

LIVEBAITING AND DEADBAITING IN STILLWATERS

Where they can be seen charging into the fry shoals during
the summer months, the usually enigmatic stillwater chub
is at its most vulnerable to a freelined or float-fished
livebait. They will take deadbaits too. Numbers of really
huge specimen chub have fallen for large deadbaits such as
whole herrings and half mackerel intended for a pike. A
friend who regularly chub fishes some of the large, deep
gravel pits adjacent to the River Thames near Oxford
actually pre-baits for chub during the winter months with
whitebait or freshly killed bleak.

A dozen or so free offerings are introduced close into the
margins along a gradual drop-off every other night (grebes
and cormorants clean them up if put in during daylight) for
a week or more, followed by several consecutive sessions
during darkness, fishing two rods with a freelined dead
bleak on each.

To ensure the 6 lb line is not bitten through by the
chub's pharyngeal teeth, the hook length is made from 10
lb test dacron to which a size 4 hook is tied. He does suffer
wonderful catches of pike in an effort to locate these
nomadic specimen chub, including the occasional whopper,
but every so often a group of chub passes through and one
succumbs to the bleak deadbait.

LURE FISHING

Working artificial lures to catch chub, particularly during
the summer and autumn, is without question one of the
most mobile and explosive ways of catching them. It is
an exploring technique where you need to be stealthy
and continually on the move and it teaches you that as
a daily part of their diet chub must eat an awful lot of
small fish.

My favourite outfit is a 5½ ft, single-handed, American bait-casting rod coupled to a baby multiplier well heeled with 8 lb test. This may seem heavy line, but it is an insurance against the odd big pike that might happen along and against the rigours of working lures through heavy weed. For the same reasons I connect the lure to a 10 lb, 6 in alasticum wire trace.

Any light-action spinning rod and small fixed-spool reel will suffice. However, on the baby American combo all chub seem like whoppers. Favourite lures are surface poppers like the crazy crawler and floating divers such as Ryobi's mugger, or Shakespeare's Big S range.

If worked erratically enough, any surface popper will persuade a chub into having a go. You impart the action by twitching it, popping, jerking, skipping it across the surface and so on. This is why the stiff little American bait-casting sticks are so good. They do not absorb your arm movements like longer, more flexible rods. All the movement is transferred into the action of the plug. Having said this, on numerous occasions when working artificials I have experienced chub coming up to grab hold of a plug that is simply being trotted downstream on the surface of a long run prior to being retrieved.

I have also used weedless crayfish imitations to good effect and I particularly love the action of buzz baits – a lightly-leaded jig to which a spoon and weed guard have been fitted, plus a propeller-type blade that churns the surface like a wounded fish. Where weed is not a problem, spinners such as the Voblex or smaller sizes of Mepps are taken greedily. Any kind of surface popping, spinning, jigging, splashing artificial lure is worth trying in both running and still waters.

FLY FISHING

The chub may well be treated by some as the poor man's trout, but in many small rivers and streams, the fly rod is yet another string to your bow and another avenue of challenge.

On the dry fly – big sedges, mayflies, craneflies (daddy long legs) – the chub offers wonderful sport, particularly at

Fly-rodding for chub is always great fun, whatever their size, because it will put the bait into water that is too shallow for any other method.

dusk and even during the heat of a summer's day when numbers of them forage between long, flowing beds of weed in search of titbits brought down by the current. When shoaled up in reasonable numbers they are not so selective as a lone brown trout, so provided your casting is accurate and the fly is cast from a downstream position so that it alights gently at the head of the run, it won't be there long.

In really streamy, broken water where heavy beds of rock or gravel are almost completely clear of weeds, the traditional wet fly cast downstream and allowed to swing across the current will take chub. Use flies with silver bodies imitative of tiny fish fry, such as the butcher, dunkeld, or teal and green, in sizes 12, 10 and 8.

For extra fun try a large, heavily weighted nymph such as the mayfly pattern, cast well upstream and twitched slowly along the bottom as it is brought back down by the current. Or what about jigging with a dog nobbler, or pulling a small spinner, spoon or tiny plug across the surface in shallow runs. They can all be presented with the fly rod (see p. 49).

In the dim light of a summer or autumn dawn almost anything plopped into the head of a chub run and twitched is liable to be taken within seconds; the chub is that obliging a fish.

Good chubbing.

INDEX